The Way It Works

The Traveler Series

by Ken Page

Clear Light Arts
United States of America

The Way It Works

Editor in Chief, The Traveler Series
Mary Darragh. Oakland, California
marydarragh@yahoo.com

Graphic design and electronic production by
Alan Klemp, Austin, Texas
aklemp@grandecom.net

First published in 1997 by:
    Clear Light Arts
    1158 Highway 105
    Boone, North Carolina 28607
    800-809-1290
    828-263-0330
    www.kenpage.com
    ken@kenpage.com

Second edition, 1999
Third edition, 2003

ISBN: 0-9649703-6-8

Dedication

This book is dedicated to all my friends and teachers of the Taos Pueblo in New Mexico.

Experiences with my Native American friends have allowed me to remember my connection to Tibet and vastly enriched my spiritual journey.

Chira G. "Sweet Medicine" Morgan gave me my Native American spiritual name, "Lightning Pole Star Warrior."

Acknowledgements

I would like to thank my friends and family for supporting me with their endless love and hard work. Without their help, I would not be the person I am today, and this book would have remained a secret.

My special thanks to Joe Nolan, who assisted tremendously in the structure and composition of this book. I thank Livea Cherish for reading the First edition and offering her insight. I thank David Michael Flatley for helping with the Second edition and Diane Cooper for her assistance and insights on the Third edition.

I would also like to acknowledge Shirley Ann Holly, my friend and co-founder of the Institute of Multidimensional Cellular Healing. She dedicated a large part of her life and energy to encouraging my dreams.

I would like to thank Mary Darragh for all the hours she worked to bring this book to completion; also, my border collie friend Rascals for her focus and conditional love which has taught me to be unconditional with personal boundaries.

Contents

Introduction

The information in this book came to me while assisting my clients to heal themselves.

Some of my ideas are different from what is currently taught in the metaphysical community. These thoughts may seem new and challenging. Perhaps there is more than one truth. I trust and follow my heart in sharing with you — that is my path.

This book may help if you are searching for wisdom about your physical, emotional, mental, and spiritual realities. I gladly share it with you unconditionally — one creator to another.

Ken Page
January 2003

Chapter 1

Why am I Here on Earth?

I wrote this book to answer the questions I hear over and over from my clients. The questions are always the same: Why am I here on Earth? What is my purpose? Why did I pick a planet and lifetime with so much pain and suffering?

Perhaps a better question is Are we creators or are we victims? Most people believe and behave as if they are victims. It is hard for them to believe they would purposely create the things that happen to them. As creators, I believe we are here on Earth to master all the conditions we, as humans, place on love. The situations we create in our lives allow us opportunities to master these conditions; I believe we return here over and over until we do master all the conditions we place on love.

Earth is a realm of dualities consisting of love at one pole and hate at the other. In between are all the other dualities we experience: War-Peace. Joy-Anguish. Hope-Despair. Happiness-Sadness. Abundance-Poverty. Betrayal-Loyalty. Beauty-Ugliness. Dualities/polarities are the dynamic fields in which we compose the lessons we create for ourselves.

If we are here on Earth to master unconditional love, do we not also have to master love's duality — hate?

> *I believe we are here on Earth*
> *to master all the conditions we,*
> *as humans, place on love.*

How many of us have mastered the love-hate duality within ourselves? How many of us hate or dislike ourselves? Or parts of ourselves? I am not sure it is possible to unconditionally love others until we first learn to love ourselves. What we can do now, however, is have unconditional compassion for others while we are learning to have unconditional love for ourselves.

In 1985, I developed a system of personal transformation called Multidimensional Cellular Healing™ (MCH™). In 1998, I opened the Institute of Multidimensional Cellular Healing™ and changed the name of my healing technique to Heart & Soul Healing™ (HSH™).

During a Heart & Soul Healing session, I assist my clients in their journey toward love, compassion, and understanding of their purpose here on Earth. The dynamics of my clients' lessons about love often originate in the past or in past lives.

Are there even such things as past lives? After doing thousands of past-life regressions, I believe there are many possible answers to that question. Whether past lives are linear or holographic lifetimes, they are the way my clients, via their subconscious minds, create stories that help them look at and understand their present lives in a different way.

I believe we are a part of Source and the collective consciousness of creation. We then collectively experience everyone's physical, mental, emotional, and spiritual realities. If this theory is true, then everything that has ever happened to anyone — anywhere, at anytime — is also a part of us.

Perhaps past-life recall is the experience of tapping

I believe we are all a part of Source and the collective consciousness of all creation.

into collective human consciousness and the archetypal stories contained there. Perhaps this concept is overwhelming because of the linear way most of us perceive our lives. So for now, let us agree that there are past lives, or at least past experiences, and that we have been on a linear path to this time and place.

How does this understanding help my clients answer the question of how they ended up here, often in the middle of so much suffering? For my client, Leslie, one of her past memories helped her to understand the dynamics she was still creating in her present life.

Leslie had a past memory as a peasant in Old Russia. Her family experienced famine, hopelessness, fear, conflict, and pain. They suffered unbearably, and she vowed, "I am going to do something about this situation if it is the last thing I ever do." What if the energy and feelings around that promise, made centuries ago, are still with her today? How would that affect her life now?

Leslie has two spiritual tasks to address in this lifetime. She needs to master unconditional love for herself and complete the promise she made in the past. She began this life by choosing her parents. The energetic patterns around them were what initially attracted her spirit. Their energies and issues were the exact reflection of the conditions she needed to master in order to evolve in her current life.

Leslie's life today mirrored her life in Old Russia. Her parents were poor, in bad health, helpless, living in a cold apartment, and unable to handle conflict. As she grew up, she blamed them for her troubled life and misfortunes. She was determined to do something about the conditions that crushed her parents and seemed to be plaguing her life as well. Although what she wanted was exactly the opposite, Leslie constantly recreated situations of

11

conflict, hopelessness, and poverty in her life, and she wanted to know why.

During her session, Leslie remembered the past-life promise she made in Old Russia and realized that to achieve the abundant, joyous life she desired for herself, she would have to balance the dualities of abundance-poverty, hope-despair, and conflict-peace within herself. Leslie realized she would be free to change her world by loving herself as she was and having unconditional compassion for her parents. This was in spite of everything she felt she lacked and disliked about herself. By addressing despair, for example, she was able to bring unconditional hope into her life.

Most of my clients, like Leslie, subconsciously continue to use the same energetic patterns, first encountered in their parents, to attract people, relationships, and challenging situations to help them learn to master unconditional love. The love-hate duality is a major life lesson we must all master in our spiritual evolution. If we master every condition we place on love, we will have unconditional compassion for all creation.

We come to Earth lifetime after lifetime and eventually experience everything that has been created. By experiencing all possible creations, we learn unconditional compassion for others — without judgment. Imagine!

Judgments create separation from others, our Creator, and ourselves. When we love ourselves unconditionally and no longer separate ourselves from Source, then those around us will have the opportunity to experience the vibration of compassion within themselves.

> *If we master every condition*
> *we place on love, we will have*
> *unconditional compassion for all creation.*

Chapter 2

Subconscious Patterns

It is apparent we have forgotten, on some level, what we came to Earth to learn and master. Even if we do not consciously remember what our lessons are, they will still be energetically drawn to us. Whatever we attract in our business and personal relationships will reflect the conditions we are here to master in this life.

We chose our parents and others in our life to help our transition from being pure spiritual energy into the physical manifestation of being human. These relationships help to guide us on our path to mastering unconditional love here on Earth. Most of us have only a few conditions left to understand in this lifetime. We test ourselves over and over by magnetically attracting certain people to reflect our issues back to us.

Our subconscious mind looks for energy patterns similar to what we need to master. The person we attract usually exhibits the energetic patterns as a mirror image of what we need to look at within ourselves.

My client Sharon, for example, needed to master her fear of taking her power. In this lifetime, she continued to attract people to her who dominated and bullied her to the point that she no longer knew what her true feelings and needs were. She felt victimized and misunderstood by her boss at work and her husband.

In our session together, she went back to a past life, in 1600 England, where she was in a life and death situation. Some people in her community feared and hated her because of her understanding of herbs and her ability to heal with her touch. Although she helped and was loved by many people in her community, she scared many others because she was different. They did not understand what she was doing and thought she was evil. The church declared her a witch, and she was taken from her home, chained up, and tortured. They made her falsely confess to evil and vile acts against her neighbors. She was a healing, loving person, but because of her service to others, she was now hurt, angry, and suffering. Since she died in the middle of these painful emotions and in a confused state, her spirit needed to understand why this happened.

Sharon understood physically what happened to her in that past life because she was accused of being a witch and evil. However, she was still confused emotionally, mentally, and spiritually. She did not understand why she was betrayed and killed for being in her passion and doing what she loved to do.

Everything that has ever happened to any one of us must be understood emotionally, mentally, spiritually, and physically. At the moment of our death, I believe we go into the Creator and the collective consciousness. We reflect on the lifetime that we just experienced to make sense of what happened.

We always come to Earth to learn or teach some form of love. In order to understand the lessons of the life we

---

*Everything that ever happened
to any one of us must be
understood emotionally, mentally,
spiritually, and physically.*

---

just left, we start at the beginning when we were with Source. We view our life like a movie and stop at every feeling and situation during its course that we did not fully understand.

In Sharon's particular past life, even though she loved what she was doing, she ended up experiencing pain, suffering, torture, and death. As a result of such confusion over many lifetimes, an aspect of her subconscious mind decided it was not safe to love, take her power, or be who she was.

Ideas like these become thought programs, and each of us has one or more deep inside our subconscious mind, playing out in our lives today. We use these energetic programs to attract other people to us to test our self-love, our personal power, and our definition of who we are. Understanding these three areas is a vital part of our spiritual journey.

> *We use energetic programs to attract other people to us to test our self-love, our personal power, and our definition of who we are.*

Chapter 3

Transforming the
Collective Consciousness

Many of us had past lives where other people projected hate and anger onto us at the moment of our death. Our reaction to these experiences varied dependent upon our sex and age. Were we male or female, young or old? If young, we were probably terrified and confused. An adult might have been angry and defiant. An older person may have been resigned. Have all these energetic feelings accumulated over time into a force of their own? Have they existed for thousands of years as the collective consciousness of fear, anger, or hate?

How many frightened and angry people in the past gave energy to the collective consciousness of war? Is it possible the collective consciousness of war maintains and compounds itself by energetically tapping into the accumulated fear and hate of people today? I believe one of our purposes here on Earth is to balance all the different collective consciousnesses — including war.

As we begin to love ourselves unconditionally and have unconditional compassion for others, could we bring the collective consciousness of war back into balance?

---

*I believe one of our purposes here
on Earth is to balance all the different
collective consciousnesses.*

By manifesting peace, balance, and unconditional love for ourselves, could others feel this and use it as a template to energetically find their own truth, freeing themselves from the pain and patterns of the past?

Because we are all One and part of the Creator, I believe we have the power to do this.

> *As we begin to love ourselves unconditionally and have unconditional compassion for others, could we bring the collective consciousness of war back into balance?*

Chapter 4

Personal Power

The most common challenge my clients, friends, and family have in connecting to the Creator and mastering all the conditions they place on love is that they have not fully stepped into their power.

Most of my clients have stopped giving their power away to others after realizing that the people they gave it to were using it against them. While in an altered state and in touch with their deepest wisdom and understanding, these people admit they are using ninety percent of their energy to stop themselves from fully taking their power. They are also using a similar amount of energy to keep themselves out of love.

If they stopped giving their power away, why would they be afraid to claim it for themselves? There are three possible answers that explain this behavior.

First, we are moving into a time of instantaneous creation when we will have a thought or feeling and our physical reality will instantly change. We are aware of this already when we imagine future events taking a specific course and they do, or we think about someone and they call on the phone. All of us have seen examples of this type of creation in our everyday lives. We are starting to know what is going to happen before it does.

We are moving into a time of instantaneous creation.

Instantaneous creation is the most common vibration shared in higher dimensions. How many of us are ready to accept the responsibility and consequences of instantaneous creation? What if your next thought and feeling created a completely different physical environment or reality? To be ready for such powerful creative skills, most of my clients realize they must be peaceful, have a quiet mind, unconditional love for themselves, feel unconditional compassion for others, and be experienced in all forms of earthly creation.

The second reason most of us are hesitant to fully take our power is that we are not clear about how our lives would change. Could we handle it? What if — right now! — you were a thousand times more powerful? How would you be? How would that feel? What would you do with such power? Would you be safe? Would others be safe?

Unless we already understood our creations — understood them physically, emotionally, mentally, and spiritually — we could be afraid we would continue to create the same patterns in the future that we created in the past. Why would we trust ourselves to create more unless we fully understood why we created our present lives — our issues, our relationships, our families, and all of our experiences?

The third reason my clients do not claim their power is they do not realize they are stand-alone creators. Most of them were taught and believe they have to co-create

---

Instantaneous creation
is the most common vibration
shared in higher dimensions.

with others and in doing so must give their power away.

If we do not realize we are all creators, each of us on our own perfect life journey, we will tend to judge the creations of others based on how we believe they should create.

The truth is, everyone's creations are absolutely perfect. We are all creating situations to help us master our issues in order to evolve and be more like Source. Who can say other peoples' realities, even if they are harsher than what we might want for ourselves, are not exactly what they need to experience to understand their life's purpose and take their power?

Only when we first become responsible creators, aware of what we create in our own lives, can we truly co-create with others.

Only when we first become responsible creators, aware of what we create in our own lives, can we truly co-create with others.

Chapter 5

Choices

Our conscious mind, which is part of the ego, holds the events, memories, and emotions experienced in this lifetime. Our subconscious mind also holds that information, plus information from other lifetimes, dimensions, and realities. Our issues are the conditions we placed on love in the past and are still dealing with today. Our issues are what we did not understand in past lives and include similar things we do not understand in this life. They make it challenging for us to have unconditional love for ourselves and unconditional compassion for others.

What we did not master in the past is drawn to us in this lifetime. Our subconscious mind recreates these issues over and over by using our energy to attract people and situations to us who reflect these issues.

One of my most important realizations was that our Higher Self, working through our subconscious mind, wants us to realize we are creating our reality, and we have choices.

When my clients ask me about their issues, I tell them that they probably experienced all of them within the past two weeks when, for example, they felt angry, hurt,

---

Our Higher Self, working through our subconscious mind, wants us to realize we are creating our reality, and we have choices.

separated, or fearful. When a situation creates one of these feelings, a person should immediately ask what this situation reveals. Simply asking this question allows the opportunity to recognize what the issues are.

My issues are clear to me. I have issues of trust, abandonment, separation, betrayal, and power and control. When I find myself in these situations, I immediately stop, step back, and observe what I am subconsciously creating. Then I no longer feel like a victim. I realize I am a creator with many choices about how I will energetically react to each situation I create.

In most cases my choice is not to give energy to the situations created by my old issues. I choose to witness them instead and watch to see what will unfold. I find it is easier to understand my creations from our collective unity consciousness where duality has no power, and I can be a witness and observer.

I can observe my life objectively from the collective consciousness and see more clearly the overall pattern of my creations. This holographic viewpoint gives me a greater understanding of the choices I make and allows me the freedom to create what I desire in my life without old patterns energetically affecting me. Each of us is able to do this. We are becoming aware we have many choices about how we will react to each situation — each moment — in our lives.

Most of us feel our lives are moving faster and time

I find it is easier to understand my creations from our collective unity consciousness where duality has no power, and I can be a witness and observer.

appears to be speeding up. In actuality, I believe time is slowing down. Perhaps time feels as if it is speeding up because we recognize what we are creating and know what is going to happen. What if our subconscious mind has been using ninety percent of our energy to recreate unresolved issues from our past? What if we recognize this fact about how we have been creating and change it? The energy we once used to recreate old patterns then becomes available for us to create what we choose to bring into our lives now.

> *The energy we once used to recreate old patterns then becomes available for us to create what we choose to bring into our lives now.*

Chapter 6

Sending Love and Light

When you are energetically out of balance and trying to help others, what really happens? Do you send love and light based on how you believe others should be or how you think they should be helped? When you send love, is it love or is it energy? These are absolutely the most important questions you need to ask yourself.

If we think we are sending love — and the receiving party does not perceive it as love but as an indistinguishable form of energy — are we intensifying and distorting another person's creation, as well as our own? Are we creating chaos and interfering when we think we are helping?

When we send any form of energy through emotion, whether it be love, care, or even thoughts of peace, can we be sure the receiving party will perceive the energy as we intend it? Does that not depend upon the state of mind of the receiver?

How can we be sure, for example, that when we send thoughts of peace to a warring country, the thought form of war does not receive that energy and become forcefully empowered by it. If we believe everything is energy then everything is also subject to the interpretation of the receiver.

What about how we perceive love? The study of Neurolinguistic Programming (NLP) talks of how each individual interprets the world through three internal modalities: visual, auditory, and kinesthetic. If you ask a visual person about God, they will see pictures. An auditory person will hear the sounds of his or her Higher Self, and a kinesthetic person will feel a sense of well-being.

By looking at the world's religions of today we can see other examples of this. How does a Christian culture send love and ideas of peace to a primarily Moslem culture? I think we would all agree that there are many different perceptions, each based on a country's history, experiences, and religious ideology.

As another example, visual people often show love for others through acts of kindness, by "doing" something special. Auditory people usually "tell" others they love them. Kinesthetic people will "touch" others to show love.

But what happens if a visual person is with a kinesthetic? Would they truly be able to communicate at the sensory level? It then becomes a matter of how each individual interprets the world and his of her ability to accept how others interpret as well.

To be more specific, does a man perceive love differently than a woman? The variables in these examples create billions of differing thoughts, ideas, and emotions. The word love is the most confusing word on the planet today, because you only know how to love based on your past experiences.

The act of sending energy is a very dynamic thing to do, and we must be cognizant of the power of this action. A huge amount of responsibility is associated with this. It is not just a benign act. You are projecting an energy wave, a force, a power, and it will affect things in a way that may not be truly felt or appreciated in the way you intend. It is like dropping a pebble into the water and the ripples fill an ant's nest on the other side of the lake. Is the act of sending love like the pebble in the water? What impact will it have outside of your own view?

Then ask yourself these questions. Do I love myself unconditionally? Do I love the way I look? My hairline? My body shape? Do I love every aspect of my life? My job? My home? My family?

When there are parts of ourselves we do not love, how can we send love and light to others? What kind of energy do we think we are sending? Will the energy we send be distorted by our own inability to love ourselves unconditionally?

What is your experience of love? Have you ever been loved completely? Did your parents love you completely? Was their love ever enough? It was not until later in life that most of us realized our parents could only love us as much as they loved themselves. Is this also true for us? Can we only love others as much as we love ourselves?

In your relationships, do you and your partner love each other equally? Most of us would say we love our partners more, hoping that as they experience our love for them, they will learn to love us more. Has this happened?

Not only do most of us not fully love ourselves, but our energetic fields are also mixed with others. I find that my clients' energetic fields are usually projected outward several hundred yards. This occurred when they were very young to possibly protect themselves from or help with family dynamics. It was safer to observe ourselves from the outside than be totally present in our body.

When our fields are projected away from our body that far, everything energetically going on around us affects our physical, mental, emotional, and spiritual bodies. When our fields are out and we send energy to

---

Ask yourself: Do I love myself unconditionally?

others who have their fields projected out also, will the collective consciousness around those that we try to help be attracted to our own energetic patterns and tap in on us, distorting our energy even further?

Sending love, light, and energy to others when we have not learned to love ourselves unconditionally will, in return, attract what we do not love within ourselves. Is there not a gentler way to learn our lessons?

What I advocate is to BE love. To BE love is to love ourselves unconditionally and have unconditional compassion for others. In this manner you do not "send" anything. You just "are." This is the beginning of the path to having unconditional love for all creation. By "being" love, others can feel this vibration within themselves, allowing them the opportunity to have more choices about how to be. Choices = Freedom.

> *To BE love is to love ourselves*
> *unconditionally and have unconditional*
> *compassion for others.*

Chapter 7

Energetic Looping

During the past few years, several people have told me they could not feel my heart. They thought something was wrong with me because I was not energetically reflecting what they wanted to feel. It took me a while to realize these people could not feel me because they were centered differently than I was. I am centered in my pineal gland. I trust and follow my heart, but I do not center myself there exclusively. I believe connecting heart to heart, the way we were taught in the past, creates energetic looping.

Energetic looping is engaging with others by projecting our issues onto them. We usually prefer to project energy from our heart or higher chakras, because we were taught these chakras are more spiritual than the lower chakras. Many of us are confused by the energies of the lower three chakras because most of our issues originated there. The first chakra, at the base of the spine, has three vibrations. It collects and projects sexual/survival, sexual/creative, and creative energy. The second chakra, or Hara point in the lower abdomen, is the point of balance for male and female energy. The third chakra, at the solar plexus, is the center of power and control.

> *Energetic looping is engaging with others by projecting our issues onto them.*

So what happens when you come from your heart? If your chakras are not balanced and you project from your heart, you also engage your lower chakras whether you intend to or not. When someone tells me they cannot feel my heart, what they are really saying and feeling subconsciously is they cannot feel themselves or what they need to look at within themselves, because I am not reflecting back their issues. Reflecting heart to heart should be a conscious decision.

When you energetically loop with others and your fields are also out, the loop will continue past the time you are with those people physically. When you see them again, the energetic patterns could still be there. They will continue to project their issues onto you whether it is guilt, anger, or pain. We all need to move out of this way of looping. This is one of the reasons I suggest clearing yourself, pulling your field back into your body, and loving yourself. I discuss this technique in the next chapter.

How is it different when you are in your space, loving yourself, compassionate towards others, and not projecting your issues? Others will not be able to loop with you in the same way because you are not projecting your issues or reflecting their issues back to them. You will recognize what your issues are and take responsibility for them without projection. You will then have a choice about how you wish to continue to learn. You can learn, instead, by witnessing others and the dynamics around you.

Most of us loop with our loved ones. We create patterns of interaction where we reflect each other's issues, and we continue these patterns of engagement to keep our loved ones attached to us. Are you afraid that if you do not reflect the issues of your loved ones they will leave you to find someone who will? Please understand that loving yourself unconditionally is very attractive.

Your loved ones will feel this wonderful energy and want to be around you, even if they do not know why. It is both healthier and easier to attract and keep a lover by loving yourself than by reflecting his or her fear and pain.

Energetically we are all changing. As our vibrations change, it will not feel good to be with some people any longer. We may not like what they are creating. We understand what they are doing and have compassion for them, yet we can choose if we want to be with them or not. By not repeating these old energetic patterns, we can accept them for what they are without judging them or ourselves.

As we fully embrace the vibration of loving ourselves unconditionally, what will happen to the people we used to loop with? They will feel the love and acceptance we have for ourselves, which will give them the opportunity to recognize this vibration in themselves and change if they choose. We can never change another person, but the more we love ourselves the easier it is for someone else to recognize that capacity within themselves.

Chapter 8

Being Energetically Clear

If you received a formula for the secret of life, such as a meditation, breathing, or clearing technique, would you neglect doing it because it was too complicated or time consuming?

I have a simple clearing technique that will change your life. It only takes a few minutes several times a day and it is easy to do. Anything that we can do physically is more powerful in our third-dimensional world.

The next time you go to the bathroom to relieve your self, use the following clearing technique in those few private moments.

TECHNIQUE FOR CENTERING, BALANCING, AND CLEARING

Whether you are sitting or standing, raise one or both hands up to the top of your head. Using your intent and focus, think "clear" as you relieve yourself and pass your hands down the front of your body imagining the old energy passing out between your legs.

Next, bring yourself into your own space by pulling in your energetic field. Start by extending your arms out from your body. Then focus your intent on being 100% in your body and draw in your arms to your solar plexus. Take another five to ten seconds to be in your space, be in the moment, and love a part of your body you dislike. You must resonate with yourself the way you resonate with something you love or enjoy. Love that part of yourself like you love a sunset or flowers. Create a feeling of comfort. Stop the exercise before your ego jumps in and tells you something different.

This process should be practiced daily. It will allow you to change your vibration and become less reactive to the projections of other people.

If you repeat this technique each time you go to the bathroom, you will consciously and quickly have the opportunity to clear your fields many times a day. Anything you do with conscious intent and focus, even if it only takes thirty seconds, will change your life and give you more choices.

KEEPING OURSELVES CLEAR WHILE WE EAT

The digestive tracts of my clients are often energetically charged with tension and worry. Were you quietly and peacefully enjoying your food the last time you had a meal or were you having an argument? Were you watching television, listening to the radio, or driving? Whatever feelings you had as you ate your meals were energetically transmitted into your food and your body.

I see people all the time that eat healthy diets. They are almost obsessed with what they can and cannot eat. Yet, while they eat they worry, read the newspaper, watch television, or do something else that has an emotional charge. The intensity of their emotions changes the vibration of the food they eat.

Imagine these scenes. You sit down to a beautiful

Anything you do with conscious intent and focus, even if it only takes thirty seconds, will change your life.

meal and watch the news on television where murders, wars, and conflicts are today's headlines. You are driving your car during rush hour traffic, eating fast food, and a fender-bender occurs right in front of you. You are having a family meal and start arguing with one of your children. What are the feelings you would be consuming during these stressful moments?

It is important to keep your thoughts clear while you eat. Think about your meal, enjoy the company of loved ones, or have a quiet moment alone until you are finished eating. This will help your digestive system and the quality of the energy you store from your food. Practice eating with a clear mind for three days and I know your life will change.

MASTERING OUR SPACE

I practice being energetically invisible. Does this sound strange? I am sure most of you have felt invisible at one time or another in your life. Being energetically invisible, however, allows us to choose how we want to use our energy and interact with others.

When most of us go to the grocery store, for example, we want to buy our groceries and leave. We want the experience to be smooth, effortless, and quick. If we pull our fields in and love ourselves before we go shopping, what will happen? If we do not reflect anyone's issues at the store, no one will see us unless we consciously and energetically choose to engage with them. Unless we make a decision to connect with someone in the store, a friend for example, we will not use any of our energy whatsoever. I believe we should save our energy for our priorities — our passions, our families — whatever we love. If we give our energy away all day long, when evening comes we are tired, have an attitude, and do not want to do anything at all. Pretty soon we stop exploring our own passions, because we gave our energy away to everyone else.

Practice shaking someone's hand and feeling nothing but his or her handshake. We should be so energetically in our own space that when we make love to our partners after they have had a bad day, this "bad day" energy will pass through us. We will feel our partners physically, but not take on any of the troubled energy. We can love them, comfort them, and be with them, and the energy of their bad day will pass through us without any negative effect.

When I start talking about pulling our fields in, loving ourselves, not sending energy, and being invisible, people become concerned. Does this mean we will never be able to be with other people and just hang out? Of course we will. It is a matter of choice. It is a matter of how we prefer to experience energy. Pulling in our fields, staying in our space, and loving ourselves allows us choices.

Pulling in our fields, staying in our space, and loving ourselves allows us choices.

Chapter 9

Loving and Creating

The more we love ourselves the easier it is for our vibration — our energetic field — to stay inside our body. If we pulled our field in and did not love ourselves, old feelings and patterns would push our spiritual essence back out. Loving ourselves is an important part of energetically staying in our space.

My clients continually ask me how they can learn to love themselves. Not many people know the answer. I tell them to begin by accepting themselves — by loving the way they look, think, and feel.

Practice loving yourself when you are happy, passionate, and blissful — when you are in your passion — whether that is writing, dancing, gardening, playing with your children, or listening to music. You can identify and embrace what loving yourself feels like in these moments of play, passion, and delight.

When you love yourself and are in your passion, all your cells vibrate with love. Being fully in your body while in your passion is a powerful way of achieving this. Moments such as making love, swimming, dancing, or playing with your family and friends allow you to feel the vibration of love throughout every cell of your body.

> *The more we love ourselves the easier it is for our vibration — our energetic field — to stay inside our body.*

These whole-body passionate moments are an opportunity to reinforce the feeling of love for ourselves. These are also the most powerful moments to create. Most of us create in a time of need — when we are out of money or in trouble. I create when I am happy and in my passion. One of the best times to generate creative energy is when we are making love or playing with ourselves and every cell in our body is ecstatic and unified.

CREATING WITH LIMITATION

I feel many of us create from a place of limitation. We create what we think we want, based on what we believe is possible for us. This is why many of the things we created in the past are now no longer what we want.

We decide, for example, we want a certain relationship and then create it. If we create from a place of limitation instead of unlimited potential, in a couple of weeks or months we will be unhappy and dissatisfied with our creation. When we do not believe we deserve the best, we end up creating relationships and other situations we never truly wanted.

QUIETING YOUR MIND

Loving yourself, creating, and being compassionate are the most important reasons for being here on Earth. Never create when you are troubled. If you have a busy mind, get physical. The more physically active you are, the quieter and calmer your mind becomes. I garden, walk, or swim when things are going a million miles a minute and my mind is too busy.

I create when I am happy and in my passion.

Another good way of quieting a busy mind is to look straight ahead and focus on something in the room. While keeping your head level, look up at the ceiling. This will immediately take you out of your emotions and quiet your mind.

RECEIVING

Receiving is an issue for most of us. Is it possible you are keeping yourself from creating the things you want because of your fears? What if you were to have everything you wanted? Do you think someone would hurt you, take what you have, or not like you anymore? Do you feel you do not really deserve it? Have you felt this way all of your life?

In the past, people close to me started receiving everything they wanted. They then subconsciously sabotaged themselves because they could not accept what they created. They could not accept having a wonderful home, relationship, or family. They could not accept a wonderful healing center or friends they could trust.

It is very important to acknowledge the positive things you create in your life and in the lives of others. The gifts of this universe are available to all of us. To overcome subconscious sabotage, acknowledge yourself as a divine creator, accept your creations, love yourself, play, and enjoy the moment.

Loving yourself, creating, and being compassionate are the most important reasons for being here on Earth.

SUMMARY

Loving yourself and being in your passion are extremely important. Both qualities assist you in staying energetically in your space and are necessary for the creative process. How many of you spend time each day loving yourself unconditionally? How many of you spend time each day being in your passion?

What if Jesus, Buddha, or Mother Mary appeared in front of you and you felt how much love they had for both themselves and for you. What if you felt how much passion they had for life? By changing your vibration to match theirs, could you heal and transform yourself?

All these wonderful healers created from a place of love and acceptance. You can love yourself. You can spend time each day with a quiet mind. You can Be, create in your passion, and accept what you have created.

You can Be, create in your passion, and accept what you have created.

Chapter 10

Giving Something Back

What should you do when you are in your space, loving yourself, and upsetting events happen in your community or someone asks for your help? Get involved. Make your compassion count by helping someone or donating time to an organization or charity. When physically helping someone or a good cause, you become more aware of your feelings, you understand yourself better, and you gain compassion for the creations of others.

We are physical beings and need to physically experience our creations. We are not victims. By helping others we affirm our compassion and gain a better understanding of being a creator and a co-creator.

LOOKING AT OUR FEARS

It is important to look at your fears as you explore your spirituality. Are you afraid of death? Are you afraid of disease? Are you afraid of failure? Are you afraid of people or of being alone? Your fears keep you out of the moment. They prevent you from fully loving yourself by energetically interfering with your ability to love those aspects of yourself. Your subconscious mind will keep energetically attracting your fears until you come to peace with them.

We are physical beings and need to physically experience our creations.

39

If you are afraid of death, volunteer at Hospice. When you work with people who are dying, you will see the beauty — as well as the pain — and come to terms with your fear of death or of being out of control.

When the changes of the future occur, I believe any fears we still have will be amplified a thousand times. Is it not better to look now, in a controlled manner, at all the things we are afraid of and find peace with these feelings? When we find peace by having unconditional love for our fearful selves, we change our vibration — and by doing so we help change the collective consciousness.

HELPING SOMEONE WHO HAS NOT ASKED FOR HELP

By energetically interfering with other people without physically asking for permission to help them, we not only take away their lessons, but we also intensify their experiences — often causing them to create something even more chaotic. Even though our intentions are well meaning and generated by love, getting caught up in the experiences of others can cause the negativity around them to rebound and affect us, too.

This can also be true when we ask someone's Higher Self for permission to assist them by sending healing energy remotely without first gaining physical agreement and participation. Because of our desire to help others, we often override our Higher Self's messages also, no matter what they are.

When we find peace by having unconditional love for our fearful selves, we change our vibration — and by doing so we help change the collective consciousness.

When people ask me if I would do a remote Heart & Soul Healing session on someone they know who has not personally asked for my help, I always tell them that I first need to do a session with them. After their session, ninety percent of the time their Higher Self tells them they should not interfere with the other person.

If we try to help people who have not physically asked us for help, I believe we intensify their creations and get caught in their experiences. Instead of trying to help others without permission, what if we have unconditional love for ourselves and unconditional compassion for them just as they are? Could they be better helped in solving their own lessons by feeling our self-love and compassion and mirroring it in themselves?

> **If we try to help someone who has not physically asked us for help, I believe we intensify their creations and get caught in their experiences.**

Chapter 11

Earth Changes

As our individual consciousness changes, so does the collective consciousness of the planet. As we love and have compassion for all creation, the vibration of the planet evolves to a higher frequency where we become less reactive to the energetics around us.

What is this changing frequency doing to our physical bodies? I believe it intensifies everything and makes time appear to be going faster. It intensifies our emotional and physical bodies and overwhelms our nervous system. During this time of change, it is important for us to truly be in the moment and not looping with others or thinking about the past.

Deepak Chopra says the average person has sixty thousand thoughts a day and ninety percent of them are thoughts of yesterday. Is it possible that by now we are full of millions of thoughts out of time? These old thoughts keep us from being present in the moment.

Everyone tells me things are going faster and faster. By being and staying in the moment, I have personally experienced that there is no time and things are slowing down. What if everything slowed down or stopped? If we were not in our passion, doing what we loved to do, I guarantee this would feel as if we were in hell.

During this time of change, it is important for us to truly be in the moment, not looping with others or thinking about the past.

When we are totally present in the moment, every experience is new. By being in the moment, we would not reference past experiences and each moment would be as if it was happening for the first time. Imagine the excitement of doing the things we love for first time: tasting chocolate for the first time, enjoying making love for the first time, dancing with ease for the first time.

If we are out of the moment and looping with the past, our issues become more chaotic. I see this everywhere. Sometimes it becomes so chaotic people want to destroy themselves or their lives. Being in the moment is the only healthy, balanced, and peaceful place to be.

DOOM AND GLOOM

Many people I know are following the different predictions of what may happen to the Earth in the near future. People are worried. People are scared. They feel they must move to a "safe" area to survive. All this fearful misinformation is creating paranoia.

It is important not to give these fears any or all of our energy. It is my belief that we, as powerful creators, could create some of these changes ourselves because of the intensity of our fears.

For every prediction of destruction, there are hundreds of other choices that we, as a collective consciousness, may choose.

In each moment, there are signs and many of them are positive. I believe if we are open to all creation, everything is a sign. We have choices in what we want to create and what we choose in our lives. If we were to ask

---

Being in the moment is the only healthy, balanced, and peaceful place to be.

---

that our spiritual lives manifest in the physical world, then all we would need to do is be aware of what is occurring around us. Everything we see would be a spiritual signpost, guiding us along our journey. We just need to get out of our heads and be more physically active.

We are about to bring in a thousand times more energy than ever before. My clients are already reacting to this increase in energy. Having healthy, active lives is challenging. We should focus on eating properly, resting, and being physically fit and active in a playful way. The weakest part of the body is the part that will blow out or implode if a person is not healthy.

What should we do to stay balanced? I believe we should love ourselves, be compassionate, pull our fields in, and stay present in the moment. We should be physically healthy, fit, and active. And most importantly, we should remember to play as we prepare for a beautiful journey.

For every prediction of destruction, there are hundreds of other choices that we, as a collective consciousness, may choose.

Chapter 12

Being in the Moment

Once we love ourselves, the next task is centering between the past and the future — in the moment. When we are compassionate and in the moment, we are free to create. The moment is the access point for the finest reflection of Source we can be.

Most of us are not in the moment. We replay past regrets, such as I wish I told my mom I loved her more before she died, I wish I finished college, or I should have been a painter instead of an accountant as my dad wanted. Or perhaps we get stuck in the future with our thoughts. When I have money, I will go back to school. When I lose thirty pounds, my life will be perfect. When I find my true love, I will finally be happy. By hanging on to past or future events or emotions, we are never truly present.

If we love ourselves and are present in the moment, a wonderful thing happens — our entire being radiates compassion. This is what I believe we are here to do. Being in the moment is the only place of true power. It is the only place where we are able to use our choices to create change. It is the place to create, overcome limitations, or change directions. Free will is the creative force of our universe.

The moment is the access point for the finest reflection of Source we can be.

GETTING TO THE MOMENT

The key to the entire process of learning, being, and creating is to stay in the moment. If someone triggers a reaction in you, they are only mirroring the issues you have come to learn and resolve. When you get thrown off center, go back in linear time and understand when and where a particular issue began for you and what you are still learning. It is important to understand the emotional charge around the issue, whether it is abandonment, self-worth, trust, guilt, shame, or power and control. Until you understand the charge around the issue, your subconscious will continue to recreate event after event so you can keep looking at what you agreed to learn.

Anytime you find yourself out of the moment, it is valuable to examine where you went — past or future — and what issue sent you there. Once you understand your issues — mentally, emotionally, physically, and spiritually — they will no longer have an energetic charge. Until you realize that you are creating a series of events to keep you focused on your issues and what you have agreed to learn in this lifetime, you will continue to subconsciously divert most of your creative energy into drawing such circumstances and people to you, thus keeping you out of the moment.

TIMELESS MOMENTS

The only place we can truly change our being is in the moment. If we are not in the moment, there will always be some form of distortion.

We are spirits having a physical experience. Spirit exists outside of time. Thinking we are bound by linear time stops us from connecting to our true holographic selves, which are multidimensional, timeless, and always in the moment.

Perhaps past and future lives are all the same. Perhaps they merely represent stories that help us understand our lives. It makes no difference whether the stories we carry around within us are real or not. What is important is to access the wisdom and understanding they contain and use it now. The real value of any information is how it enriches and supports our lives today and helps us to understand more about ourselves.

By accessing this timeless state within our cellular being, we access self-knowledge and wisdom. Being in the moment, centered in the pineal (see Chapter 22), allows us to immediately access the original traumatic events that set up the issues for us in this life.

Many times we are unable to stay in the moment because past events were so overwhelming and painful they continue to confuse and disturb us today. The pain of what happened causes our subconscious minds to block the real truth of the event. Heart & Soul Healing techniques uncover and integrate the information we need. Our conscious mind then understands mentally, emotionally, physically, and spiritually what the lesson was, and we are free to be fully in the moment.

MISSING PARTS

How can you be present in the moment if you are not fully in your body? Many of you decided to protect yourself energetically by getting out of your body because you were violated and hurt in the past. In session, most all of my clients say ninety percent of their

> *By accessing this timeless state within our cellular being, we access self-knowledge and wisdom.*

essence is missing. By the age of three, most of my clients left their body by saying, "I do not want to be here." Today, they are so full of past feelings and emotions that they do not know how they truly feel.

The missing parts of us are with the collective consciousness observing, learning, understanding, and becoming aware. Our task is to bring these missing parts back into our physical body and be totally conscious and present in the moment.

Our task is to bring these missing parts back into our physical body and be totally conscious and present in the moment.

Chapter 13

Pattern Release Technique

I want to share a powerful technique for releasing old energy patterns that are keeping you out of the moment. A good time to use this technique is while taking a bath. Plan for fifteen to thirty undisturbed minutes.

Take off your jewelry, including your rings. Light a candle to represent a spiritual person you admire. Picture them with you. Say your name first, then the name of the spiritual person, such as Krishna, Sai Baba, Moses, Jesus, Mother Mary, or Buddha. Feel the unconditional love this spiritual person reflects and recognize that place of love inside you.

Stare at the flame and release old feelings, thoughts, programs, issues, and fears. Allow them to flow through you. Say them either out loud or in silence. Your intention to clear yourself is most important.

Begin by releasing the things you are afraid of, such as losing your job, getting older, poverty, illness, or being alone. Next release thoughts, feelings, and emotions you are holding, such as guilt, anger, sorrow, or sadness. Release feelings of being helpless, hopeless, used, or trapped. Release feelings of pain and jealousy. Release all the feelings and projections of others that you have bought into. During the release, make an intention to keep the wisdom gained from these events and feelings.

Next, I want you to do something different. I want you to release all the positive memories you are holding on to from your past. Are you holding on to the best

49

Christmas you remember? Or the best present you ever received? Your first car or favorite home? Your first great love? Your proudest moment? A happy time with your family? Food, sunsets, flowers — release them all.

How many of you are holding these positive past events and feelings and using them to judge every experience you create today? Are you comparing every kiss or embrace today to an experience you had in the past? Release every positive experience from your past that is keeping you from being in the present moment and experiencing things for the first time.

During the release, make an intention to keep the wisdom, joy, and love from these positive past events. All you are doing is releasing the energetic charges you are holding on to that are causing you to have judgments and comparisons today.

Once you have released all the charged negative and positive experiences from your past, shower or bathe with fresh water.

Positive experiences often have more of an energetic charge than our fears. Think about it. We do our best to heal the negative things from our past, but we do not realize we are also comparing positive experiences. Releasing all charged memories is a helpful technique to aid us in staying present in the moment.

Positive experiences often have more of an energetic charge than our fears.

Chapter 14

INscension™

Until we are fully present and conscious here on Earth, I believe we are not going anywhere. How could we move into another dimension if we have not yet mastered this dimension? INscension™ is being fully present in our body with conscious awareness.

Let us talk about this dimension. I believe many of us act like two-dimensional beings in a three-dimensional reality. The two-dimensional aspects of our reality are the dualities such as good-evil, light-dark, positive-negative, and male-female. Our third dimension is more than we have been led to believe. If we are fully present and in the moment here — if we achieve INscension — we will be able to connect with all other dimensions and realities right now because our third-dimensional world is holographically connected to everything.

One reason I believe our dimension is holographic is because other dimensional beings are here asking us for assistance. Why would they be doing this? Why is the third dimension so important? I believe the main reason is that when we are in the moment we are able to collapse time and affect other realities.

> *INscension™ is being fully present in our bodies with conscious awareness.*

THE END OF TIME

As we learn to be present we may reach the end of time that many of us have heard about. Maybe the end of time is simply moving into the timeless state of the moment and being present in our body. When we are in the moment, we are timeless. What if the true gift of having a physical body is to provide us with a constant anchor point for the moment?

The quality of the moment should never be underestimated. When I am fully in the moment I am no longer certain I have past lives; they no longer have an emotional charge for me.

I believe this lifetime and all past lifetimes are collapsing into the moment. Instead of past lives, I now simply have memories that are part of my wisdom and understanding. It no longer matters whether these experiences were on this planet or other planets, or whether they occurred yesterday or will happen tomorrow.

When we are in the moment, we are gates to the Creator and every dimension of reality.

Maybe the end of time is simply moving into the timeless state of the moment and being present in our body.

Chapter 15

The Void

Dualities such as love and hate are collapsing and dissolving. The collective consciousness, which feeds on these dualities, is also starting to collapse. Everything is changing, evolving, and moving away from the polarities of light and dark towards clear light where all dualities balance.

As dualities collapse, so do our realities. The collapse of dualities makes life appear to be going faster. These changes create pressure on us, our lives, and on the Earth. As dualities collapse we are being pushed into another vibrational space — the Void.

The Void is around us all the time and has many color stages. The first stage can be perceived when your meditative space turns a golden hue. The gold vibration then becomes orange, then burnt umber, and finally a transparent black. The Void is easy to see at night. Some see a translucent black mist when they first wake up, still half asleep and groggy. This is the Void.

The Void is the gate between this reality and the next dimension, a dimension of instantaneous creation. It has been described as both completely neutral and totally reflective. What we may face in the Void, multiplied one thousand times, are any remaining fears or pieces of our

---

As dualities collapse, so do our realities.

---

own inner dualities/polarities that we have yet to bring into balance. To pass through the Void we must face our worst fears.

What would facing your fears feel like? Imagine standing in front of a gigantic black mirror. Your fears — your remaining issues — are reflected in the mirror and amplified a thousand times back to you. What if you were afraid? Could you walk through this reflection?

Could you even run the other way now that the collective consciousness and Earthly dualities have changed? What if you were to feel unconditional love for yourself and amplify that feeling a thousand times? Is this what the Creator feels like?

LYING   *U. of Va. Study*

The Void reflects all distortions in our lives. Besides our fears, lying is also a main cause of distortion. A study of college students at the University of Virginia revealed that lying seems to be a way of life for many people. The results showed the students told lies in seventy-seven percent of all conversations with strangers, forty-eight percent with acquaintances, and twenty-eight percent with their best friends. They lied to their lovers thirty-four percent of the time. Lies to Mom came in at forty-six percent. This included "small lies" told to protect other people's feelings. We can see how easy it is to get confused about our own truth.

A survey of one thousand adults reported in the book, *The Day America Told the Truth*, found ninety-one percent lie routinely and fifty-nine percent admitted lying regularly

---

> **To pass through the Void**
> **we must face our worst fears.**

---

to their kids. In a survey published in the April 4, 1997 edition of *USA Today*, forty-eight percent of workers admitted to unethical or illegal acts in the workplace.

These reports reveal that the average person lies twice a day. With each lie we create a barrier making it more difficult to know our truth. This in turn disconnects us from our ability to tap in on our psychic senses and causes distortion in our connection to our Creator.

I believe one of the most important prerequisites to having a clear mind and using all our psychic abilities is to always be truthful. When we lie, we cover our true feelings. We hide our truth so the other person will not know we are lying. Does hiding our true feelings from others also hide them from ourselves and separate us from the Creator?

Lying confuses us and distorts our perceptions of reality. Lying causes us to distrust our feelings, creating separation and miscommunication with our Higher Self. One of the requirements of mastering unconditional love for ourselves and all creation is to be honest.

TRUST VERSES LIKE

Experts say we trust what is familiar. Is it possible we attract to ourselves what we trust and are familiar with, such as the way our father or mother acted, even though we do not like those behaviors? What we trust is not necessarily what we like; it is what we survived.

To know if this is true for you, look at what you do not like about your parents. Perhaps your mother was

---

Lying causes us to distrust our feelings, creating separation and miscommunication with our Higher Self.

---

angry and mean. Do you still have a pattern today of attracting angry and mean women? One reason for continuing this pattern would be you subconsciously feel comfortable with anger because you survived it in your past. In other words, you trust angry women because that is what you grew up with, even though you do not like being around angry people.

Conflicting feelings like these become highly distorted in the Void and can bring up many confusing emotions. These confusing emotions can make us feel like we are out of control or going crazy. A quiet mind will allow these momentary feelings to pass through us so that they will not be recreated in the space of the Void.

As we prepare ourselves to pass through the Void and enter the dimension of instantaneous creation, we will be tested. We will be tested by having to face our worst fears. Our fears and any distortions we have in our lives will be reflected back to us a thousand times by the Void. Having a quiet mind, loving ourselves, being physically healthy, and being in the moment will allow us safe passage through the Void and into the next dimension.

Chapter 16

Communicating with Our Higher Self

Many people tell me they cannot communicate with their Higher Self. They do not trust what they hear or feel from their own inner voice — if they hear one at all — and so they seek answers about their lives from others.

How does our Higher Self communicate with us? Most of us communicate with our Higher Self through our subconscious mind using a major sensory modality — we see, hear, or feel. If we are having a conversation with someone who needs to visualize information, while we need to feel things, we could easily misunderstand each other even if we are expressing the same idea. Many of us are kinesthetic — we feel the answers from our Higher Self with our whole body, but others may see or hear their information.

Trusting our feelings is a problem for many of us. We do not trust or listen to our feelings or our inner voice because of past situations when we have been hurt. The first feelings or impressions that come to us, however, are messages from our Higher Self and need to be honored and trusted.

Most of us communicate with our Higher Self through our subconscious mind using a major sensory modality — we see, hear, or feel.

I have a simple exercise to connect you with your Higher Self. Once you are familiar with this technique you can use it confidently to answer any questions about your life. You do have all your answers within you.

For this exercise, sit at a table with paper and pen. First, clear and quiet your mind by focusing on a point on a wall straight ahead. Hold your head level and shift only your eyes so you are looking up at a point on the ceiling. This will quiet your mind immediately and take you out of your emotions.

When your mind is quiet, write down the question "Why am I here on Earth?" Then ask the question quickly three times, either to yourself or out loud:

Why am I here on Earth?
Why am I here on Earth?
Why am I here on Earth?

Always write down the first word that comes to you. The answers may come as words, pictures, or feelings. Some of the words you may get are love, teach, learn, play, heal, or share. It could also be a word that does not make sense. Do not judge it, just go on with the exercise.

If the answer is "to love," find out what it really means by writing another question to your Higher Self. Whatever the words were that you received, write the next question using these words, always pertaining to why you are here on Earth. Ask, for example, how do I love? How do I teach? How do I heal? What does love mean? What am I supposed to be teaching? What am I supposed to share? Always keep your questions simple and use as few words as possible.

As you write your question, clear your mind and repeat the question three times — out loud or in your mind — just as you did the first time. Then write down your answer again.

Perhaps the sequence went like this:
Why am I here on Earth? To love.
What does love mean? It means to take your power.
What does taking my power mean?

Continue this process using the key words from your answer to create a new question. Write down everything that comes to you even if it is strange. Go as fast as you can and do not think about it. Keep writing and asking questions until you start to write continuously.

Do this for five minutes and then look at what you have written. Your answers will give you the key to why you are here on Earth and what you have been creating. You can use this same process to answer any questions you have.

In Heart & Soul Healing sessions, I put my clients in touch with their Higher Self. They already know all their own answers. They just need to trust.

In Heart & Soul Healing sessions, I put my clients in touch with their Higher Self. They already know all their own answers. They just need to trust.

Chapter 17

Lucid Dreaming

We are moving into the dimension of instantaneous creation and preparing for a major shift in our consciousness. Much of the preparation for these changes is happening in our dream state. The dream state is another dimension. Through our dreams, we can create and explore new realities and dimensions of consciousness. Lucid dreaming is a technique that can help us prepare for this shift.

Lucid dreaming is a powerful creative state and can be used for understanding and creating our lives. It is one of the most important techniques I practice. Research at Stanford University indicates lucid dreaming occurs during REM (rapid eye movement) sleep. Since most REM sleep takes place in the later part of the night, mornings are likely to be the most favorable time for lucid dreaming.

I have a simple and effective exercise to improve your ability to lucid dream. In this exercise you will discover if any hidden programs or ideas in your subconscious mind are keeping you from having what you desire in this life. After you have perfected your ability to lucid

> *We are moving into the dimensions*
> *of instantaneous creation . . .*
> *Much of the preparation for these changes*
> *is happening in our dream state.*

dream and have a good understanding of the subconscious patterns affecting your ability to create in the third dimension, you can go a step further and use lucid dreaming to explore other dimensions and realities.

To begin the lucid dreaming exercise, first think of a question about your life. Your question may concern a special relationship, spiritual goals, your health, or your job. Whatever it is, write it down. Keep your questions simple and use as few words as possible. Complicated questions will create complicated dreams filled with too much information to easily understand.

After choosing a simple question, set your alarm clock for half an hour earlier than you would normally get up in the morning. Use the type of clock with a snooze alarm that goes off every ten minutes. When the alarm goes off, press the snooze alarm button, focus on your question, and fall back to sleep. In the following dream, your subconscious mind will show you stories representing the ideas or programs you subconsciously carry that are related to your question. These stories will help you understand the programs that are keeping you from having what you want. After ten minutes, the alarm will go off again. Notice briefly what you were dreaming, ask the same question, and fall back to sleep. Continue doing this for thirty minutes.

After thirty minutes either tape record or write down the information you received while it is still clear in your mind. Since dreams can slip away so quickly, have a recorder or pad and pencil ready by your bed. You do not have to record the complete dream, just the main ideas and images.

The more you practice lucid dreaming, the easier it becomes. Keep asking the same question until you get a clear, understandable answer and then ask another question. Within two weeks you should uncover and understand the subconscious programs you have that are interfering with your creations.

One of the first questions I explored though lucid dreaming was How do I become a good healer and teacher? Through lucid dreaming I discovered my subconscious mind held the idea that if I became popular as a healer I would lose my freedom because I would attract attention. I was surprised at this information. My freedom is important to me, but I did not think my need for freedom would interfere with being of service to others. My subconscious mind was doing everything it could to keep me from being as successful as I was capable of being because it did not want me to lose my freedom.

By becoming conscious of my subconscious program, I was able to change it. I now understand what personal freedom means to me, and I know it is safe to become popular without losing my freedom. By exploring the dimension of lucid dreaming, I was able to become aware of the hidden, subconscious programs affecting my success.

My dream state now feels as real to me as my waking physical state. If I do not understand what is going on in my dreams or they contain problems and conflicts, I continue to replay the same dream over and over until I do understand and the conflicts are resolved. If I create perfection in my dreams by understanding and resolving any conflicts, I can use this insight to create a more balanced and healthy physical reality for myself.

By exploring the dimension of lucid dreaming, I was able to become aware of the hidden, subconscious programs affecting my success.

Lucid dreaming is a powerful technique because it assists us in understanding our subconscious mind. By practicing lucid dreaming we can be sure our subconscious mind fully supports our conscious mind in creating what we choose.

With lucid dreaming, we can perfect being in the dimension of instantaneous creation, and then we can bring this mastery to our three-dimensional lives. Lucid dreaming is one of the most important exercises we can do — it allows us a greater understanding of our lives and our universe.

With lucid dreaming, we can perfect being in the dimension of instantaneous creation, and then we can bring this mastery to our three-dimensional lives.

Chapter 18

Guides and Angels

At the beginning of your spiritual path you probably heard about getting messages from your guides and angels. Many people connect with religious guides, such as Mother Mary, Saint Germaine, or Archangels Michael and Gabriel. I believe guides and angels are aspects of us co-existing in other realities or vibrations.

If you recognized a guide as an aspect of yourself, would you take it seriously? Would you not listen and pay closer attention to a guide that appeared in a form you regarded highly? Is it easier for you to trust an outside form or idea more than one of your own?

To communicate with guides and angels you must understand how you perceive information. Many of us are kinesthetic — we receive information through whole-body feeling. Messages from guides, angels, or other aspects of us are so gentle and pure that sometimes they are difficult to feel when our minds are busy.

An effective way to quiet a busy mind is to be physically active and then relax. Afterwards, you will feel more connected and quiet in your mind and it will be easier to hear messages from your guides and angels.

Some of us hear our guides and angels very clearly

I believe guides and angels are aspects of us co-existing in other realities or vibrations.

and have even made major life changes based on these messages; the messages received were powerful, beneficial, life affirming, and felt right even though the whole picture may not always have been understood.

Some people, however, have also made changes in their lives based on what their angels told them and the information they received did not feel right or make sense. They believed the information was from a higher source and must be right. Such information was not from their guides or angels; it was from an aspect of their fears and ideas. Many times my clients have described angelic beings and these beings proved to be something entirely different when we looked more closely. Your angels would not tell you to hurt yourself, put yourself in danger or hardship, or do something physically or financially destructive. You must always use discernment about information you receive and subsequent actions you take.

I tell a story in my book, *The End of Time*, about an old girlfriend of mine who got a message from a "spiritual guide." She had gone to a new massage therapist and had a profound spiritual experience. She wanted me to have a massage the next day with the same woman. Although she did not tell me the details of her experience, I agreed to go.

As I was having the massage, a strange energy came into the room and really frightened the massage therapist. This same energy had come in the day before and taken

---

Your angels would not tell you to hurt yourself, put yourself in danger or hardship, or do something physically or financially destructive.

---

on the illusion of what my girlfriend believed was a high spiritual being. The being mirrored this illusion back to her, thus disguising its destructive nature. It took on the appearance of Jesus and told her to let me go romantically and "give me" to the massage therapist. Although we were very much in love, she listened to this message even though it felt wrong, because she thought the message came from "Jesus." The energy being was really dark, and I ended up energetically clearing the negative energy enveloping this being.

MY GUIDES AND ANGELS

I had many guides and angles at the beginning of my spiritual path, and they were enormously valuable to me. Amy, a wonderful psychic friend from São Paulo, Brazil, helped me contact them. I asked her who my guides were, and after she meditated for seven days she told me I had twelve guides. She gave me their names, when and where they had lived, and why they had come to assist me.

Moses was one of my first guides. Wow, I could not believe it! Everyone in my metaphysical community at that time believed a guide like Moses could only be with one person at a time. Now, of course, I know this is not true. Over the next year my guides, and new ones who came in, showed themselves to me. They represented many different paths of healing. I had guides from the Hawaiian kahuna tradition. Saint George, the dragon slayer, was one of my guides. I also had many holy guides from India, several from the American Indian path, and some sophisticated psychic guides from England.

I made a detailed chart depicting my guides in teams depending upon how I thought they should work together.

After completing the chart I felt a pulling sensation on my auric field. Did another guide want to come in? I went to Amy and talked with her. She also felt another guide and helped me to make contact. It was the Egyptian pharaoh Ramses II. I was very confused. I had Moses already, why would I want Ramses II, considering the energy the two had created when they battled over the release of the Hebrew slaves? I said to Ramses, "Just give me one good reason why I would allow you to be my guide when I have Moses here already?" The answer came in very clearly. "We want you to help us heal what we started a long time ago in Egypt."

His answer overwhelmed me. Then I realized that my guides were using me just as I was using them. There was an equal exchange of experiences, feelings, and emotions. Until then, I thought my guides and angels knew everything and I knew nothing. Guides need to experience and understand, just as we do, to continue evolving.

I continued working with my guides and angels in different situations. The 1991 war in the Middle East broke out at this time, and I was told how my guides and I could help. After completing my job, I realized I did not need my guides and angels in the same way. I set them free to be with others. I told them to come back anytime there was new information or they needed my assistance.

When I released my guides and angels, I started getting a different kind of communication — one from my Higher Self, the angelic God part of me. I realized my

---

Guides need to experience and understand, just as we do, to continue evolving.

guides and angels were all aspects of myself. I also realized there was no separation, and I had the information
inside me all along.

> *I realized my guides and angels were all*
> *aspects of myself. I also realized there was*
> *no separation, and I had the information*
> *inside me all along.*

Chapter 19

Walk-ins

A walk-in experience is commonly defined as a soul leaving a person's body and another soul coming in and taking over. Walk-ins are also known as aspect shifts or dimensional overlays. Ruth Montgomery talks about walk-ins in her books, *Companions Along the Way* and *Strangers Among Us*. Several people I know say they have had this experience, including my uncle, Drunvalo Melchezidek.

If your soul left and another soul came in and replaced it, would this not feel like a complete death and rebirth? Do not all of us experience this during times of great spiritual and psychic change? There are many definitions of the walk-in experience, and I believe that each of us is a walk-in. Ask yourself the question Is there a part of me with Source? What if you became conscious of the part of you with Source, and it became conscious of you? Might both aspects of you start exchanging energy and could you then experience both realities? What if there is an aspect of you existing in every other dimension, plane, or reality?

Once you became conscious and love yourself completely, could you be aware of these other aspects, these reflections of yourself, and start integrating them in this physical world? Integrating them continuously would feel like a cycle of death and rebirth. Maybe we are all continually having walk-in experiences with aspects of ourselves.

Most of us believe we are part of Source or Creator. Being part of Source means we are part of all things. Yet do we not want to separate ourselves from people and things we do not like or accept? Most of us do not want to admit there could be the energy of war or hate within us. Keeping ourselves separate from anything separates us from Source. To reconnect to all aspects of us we must love and accept all creation, because all creation is part of us.

MY EXPERIENCE

I had my first conscious walk-in experience in 1987, and it changed my life. I became aware of three aspects of myself existing simultaneously: a Native American named Juan Concha, a space being from another dimension, and an aspect of the dolphin and whale consciousness. When I became aware of these other parts of me, I knew I was multidimensional. As more aspects of me came into my consciousness, I knew that there was no separation and we are all One.

There are many times in our life when I believe a part of our essence or soul follows a loved one who has passed to understand where they are going. These times are gates or openings that make it easier to enter into other dimensions.

In the early eighties, I often traveled to Taos, New Mexico, to see a good friend, Cradle Flower, who was from the Taos Pueblo. My uncle, Drunvalo, also lived near Taos, so one day I went to visit him. He was living in a secluded area, surrounded by fields of sage. Since Drunvalo is only four years my senior, I thought of him as my brother. I had grown up knowing him as Donny.

I will never forget sitting there and talking with him that day. He told me Donny had died in Canada in 1972 and a

---

Maybe we are all continually having walk-in experiences with aspects of ourselves.

---

new soul had come in. This new soul was named Drunvalo Melchezidek. I did not know what to think. At the time, I was an entrepreneur and businessman and had not done any metaphysical or spiritual exploring. So there I sat, in my three-piece suit, questioning my whole reality and feeling sad about the loss of my brother.

In 1995, I was in Georgia at a conference with Drunvalo and several other speakers when I suddenly understood this experience. I realized part of me, during our earlier conversation in Taos, had energetically gone searching for Donny.

I found him in a different reality, the Melchezidek vibration. Since that time I have been communicating with him in that vibrational dimension, as well as channeling an aspect of myself that is also there. The closer I got to where my uncle had energetically gone, the more information I received about our soul's journey and the role of walk-ins. By staying in the moment and constantly changing my vibration, I have bridged that reality.

I now know I am a Traveler. I have become the Clear Light vibration of the Melchezidek Order, the Great White Brotherhood, and the Order of the Messiah. A messenger.

We can all have these experiences. Every one of us is starting to bridge these realities and become all we can be.

I now know I am a Traveler. I have become the Clear Light vibration of the Melchezidek Order, the Great White Brotherhood, and the Order of the Messiah. A messenger.

Chapter 20

Channeling

What is a medium or channel? Channeling is a method of communicating with beings, entities, spirits, or divine messengers. The entity or spirit partners with a physical person who gives voice to the thoughts and insights of the channeled being.

Who or what is actually being channeled? Are these aspects of the channeler or are they really beings — St. Germaine, Jesus, Michael the Archangel, or extraterrestrials — as the channeler claims? If I were to channel my guides, acknowledging they were aspects of myself, would anyone listen? Would you listen if I said, "I am now going to channel Ken Page's Higher Self"? Would you not rather pay attention to someone who said, "I channel Michael the Archangel"?

Some of these channeled beings often have brilliant and insightful messages that greatly enhance our spiritual lives. Some do not. I believe hate, fear, and cruelty do not exist in higher vibrations. Source is pure love and so are the higher vibrations where dualities do not exist.

We must have discernment when listening to different channels and notice whether the beings they channel are fearful or cruel. Does the channeled being say things that hurt others or are not congruent with our perceptions of

> **Source is pure love and so are the higher vibrations where dualities do not exist.**

love? If they do, are the channels merely sharing aspects of themselves or a particular being filtered and distorted through the dualities of their own reality?

I know people who have changed their lives — moved, left their families, quit their jobs — to follow a person who was channeling a being from another time or reality. They found out later that different interpretations of the information coming in were made by the physical channel based on what the channel needed for his or her own life, ego, or survival. When channels start modifying messages or incorporating their own ideas when communicating a feeling, which is challenging to express in words, the message may become distorted.

I worked once in an area of the United States where a well-known channel had lived and worked for several years. The channel's center had several thousand students in a multi-level school. The students had to take a pledge of secrecy regarding the teachings.

After I had done two workshops in this community and was becoming fairly well known, I planned to return for a third workshop. I checked the school's calendar to be certain they did not have any activities scheduled for the same weekend as my workshop. As soon as I set the dates and mailed out my brochures, all the student levels were called in for a "special teaching" on the exact dates I had chosen.

Was this intentional? Was my coming to town a threat? How could that be? What was I sharing that concerned them? A high-ranking individual in the school explained the situation to me. They did not want their students to attend my workshop, because I was sharing some of the exact material their leader was channeling and that created a problem for them. Since I am "just a normal man," and I had this information, they

73

were concerned that each one of the students would discover that they, too, had this information inside them. They would no longer need to listen to a being channeled from another reality for insight.

I think it is important for channels to acknowledge they are bringing forth a unique aspect of themselves. This does not make their information any less valuable.

Giving our power away, however, to an outside source that identifies itself as a "higher being" is dangerous, especially if the being is filled with confusion, anger, jealousy, or fear. These are not the vibrations of higher realities. They are the vibrations of people communicating from realities and places that are potentially less evolved than our own. It is important not to give our power away. All of our answers are within us already.

It is important not to give our power away. All of our answers are within us already.

Chapter 21

Being Energetically Healthy

Many people come home to their families after working all day at stressful jobs where there are arguments, angry people, constant deadlines, and long hours. These people often come home energetically exhausted and yet they want their families to meet and accept them as they are — even though they have the vibrations from the day all over them.

After being exposed to highly charged energies, it is important to bathe and change your clothes as soon as you get home. You want to be energetically clean when you rejoin your family. Doing this will make an enormous difference in interactions with your loved ones and others.

Most people shower in the morning. They go to bed at night energetically wearing everything that they were exposed to during the day. The next morning, as they head for the shower, they are often exhausted and wonder why they did not have a restful sleep. There are many energies out there that most of us would not want to hug or take to bed.

After being exposed to highly charged energies, it is important to bathe and change your clothes as soon as you get home.

For those in the healing professions, it is vital to change your work clothes at the end of the day. Any clothes we wear all day absorb energy. It helps not to mix the clothes you take off with the rest of the clothes in your closet. Keep your work clothes separate, so your closet and the rest of your clothes will not vibrate with unwanted energy. I put my dirty clothes in a plastic sack. The plastic will contain the old energy. When it is time to do the laundry, I put them in with the rest of my clothes to be cleaned.

Many people do not clean their jewelry every day, either. They wash themselves and clean their clothes, but they wear the same jewelry day after day without taking it off and intentionally cleansing it. Metal jewelry attracts and conducts energy. As energy moves down your hand and all around you, a ring filled with built-up energy can block your energy flow and cause pain in your shoulders, neck, or back. When you shower at night, slip off rings and other jewelry. Run water over them and think "clear," so your intention can energetically clear them.

The other day I worked with a woman who wore diamond earrings. I asked her when she last took them off and cleaned them. She said it had been a week or two. There was so much energy built up in those diamonds that her ears ached, her hearing was affected, and she had headaches. I told her she had to clean her jewelry every day, especially if she wore crystals or stones over her heart area. All of these things pick up energy. Metals will buffer the energy until they are full, and then they will reverse and send the energy back out.

The same is true for people who wear a leather belt for years. Leather is organic and picks up energy. When you put on an old belt, are you strapping on the energy of all the past times you wore it?

I teach a simple method to clear leather belts and other leather items. To make sure you do not take any of the energy you are clearing from the leather into your body, place a rubber band just below your elbow on your clearing hand. For men, your clearing hand is your right hand. For women, it is your left. The rubber band is used to remind you to keep the energy below your elbow.

Hold the belt buckle with one hand and grasp the belt with your clearing hand. While aware of your intention to clear, pull the built-up energy out of the leather by pulling your clearing hand along the entire length of the belt five to ten times. When finished, wash your hands while thinking "clear."

The easiest thing to do if you are involved in healing work or have a stressful job is to wear a cloth belt or rotate leather belts. The same is true for leather shoes. Rotating leather belts and shoes allows the leather to energetically release some of the charge it has picked up. This is also true for leather wallets and purses, especially if you have carried the same one for years. Clear any leather item just as you would a belt.

One of the most highly charged pieces of clothing I ever saw was a leather jacket worn by a teenager in Canterbury, England. His mother brought him to me for a Heart & Soul Healing session. When he came into the room, his leather jacket was a vibrating energetic life force all its own. He wore the jacket day and night, indoors and out. He wore it to school; he wore it to nightclubs. I ended up clearing the jacket before his session even started.

It is not easy to clear some items, such as feather or down pillows and comforters. I once used a down pillow in my healing work to release energetic patterns from my clients. Afterwards, I did everything I could to clear it. I took it to the dry cleaners and left it out in the sun, and it still carried an energetic buzz from all the thoughts and patterns of the healing sessions. I ended up throwing the pillow away.

Have you slept on the same down pillow for the last ten years? What if you and your partner had arguments or emotional exchanges while in bed? Is it possible that feelings and emotions leave imprints in the feathers of your down pillow or bedding? The quills of the feathers store energy because they were once alive. If you had a love relationship end, I suggest you do yourself a favor and buy new bedding.

Crystals also pick up and transmute energy. Many people I know, especially healers, have crystals in their healing rooms and throughout their homes. If you are not cleaning your crystals at least once a week, they will begin to give off the energy that they have picked up over time. The environment around the crystals may also start to feel bad or become chaotic. I suggest you keep just a few crystals in your healing room or bedroom, and clean them often with running water and your intention.

Remember that your intention is the most important part of energetic clearing. Some people suggest using sea salt or sage as a clearing method, but I find sunlight or running water and your intention to clear works just as well.

Remember, your intention is the most important part of energetic clearing.

Chapter 22

The Pineal Gland

In the previous chapters of this book, I presented the best of what I know. More information is coming in all the time. In this chapter, I would like to share with you the way much of this information came to me and introduce you to knowledge and methods that will allow you to get your own answers. I believe the most valuable knowledge is centered in the pineal gland. This includes information from Creator, Mother Earth, direction from guides and angels, wisdom from your Higher Self, and communications from extraterrestrials.

The pineal is a tiny and powerful gland, crucial to the healthy functioning of your physical, mental, emotional, and spiritual bodies. Just a little bigger than a grain of wheat. The pineal is about one quarter inch long, reddish-gray, and shaped like a cone. It is located in the middle of the brain between the right and left lobes, behind and just above the pituitary gland, and attached to and situated over the third ventricle of the brain. You can imagine its location by drawing a straight line from a point between your eyebrows to the back of your head, then drawing another straight line above your ears. Picture the pineal gland down in the middle of the brain where the two lines intersect.

While we are most interested in the spiritual functioning of this special gland, knowledge about its physical, emotional, and mental activities will also be useful, because if the pineal is not physically healthy nothing is

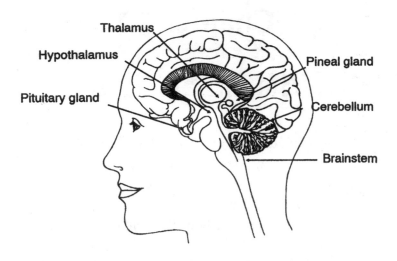

Thalamus

Hypothalamus

Pituitary gland

Pineal gland

Cerebellum

Brainstem

From *Awaken Healing Light of the Tao*,
by Mantak & Maneewan Chia. Drawing by Juan Li.

going to work right. If it has not been activated, I believe practicing the Living Light Breath™ (Chapter 24) can help restore the pineal gland to good working order.

The pineal gland is part of the body's endocrine system and produces regulatory substances called hormones that are transmitted by the bloodstream to different cells and organs. Scientists consider the pineal to be the master gland, "the regulator of regulators" that insures the proper rhythm of the hormonal and cellular systems. The pineal gland secretes a vital hormone called melatonin, which modulates and fortifies the immune system and stabilizes the nervous system. It induces sleep, gives you energy and strength, and is an aphrodisiac and thyroid stimulator. Melatonin is also the body's main antioxidant, preventing damage to the cells and DNA; it is an anti-aging, anti-cancer, anti-stress, and anti-insomnia hormone.

Melatonin regulates the circadian rhythms — the day and night cycles — of the body's metabolism. It is released into the bloodstream at night in darkness, and production stops at sunrise. If you sleep with a light on, you may be interfering with the natural production of melatonin.

The pineal produces melatonin from serotonin. Serotonin is a neurotransmitter. It allows energy to bridge the gap between nerve cells. Serotonin is most highly concentrated in the pineal. As you grow older, the balanced flow of these vital fluids may be disturbed because the pineal gland starts to calcify. As the pineal calcifies, melatonin production decreases.

The calcification of the pineal gland and decrease in melatonin output activates the body's aging process. Autopsies done on those who died with Alzheimer's disease showed substantially decreased melatonin levels. In the West, women with breast cancer have reduced pineal activity and high pineal calcification. Breast cancer is not common in Japan, where middle aged women have very low calcification of the pineal gland.

I practice the Living Light Breath to assist me staying centered in my pineal gland. I continuously draw spiritual light into my pineal to reverse calcification and keep this gland healthy and fortified. Anyone can easily learn to do this. And when you do, I believe you will remain healthy and youthful, and will enjoy the benefit of increased spiritual communication, connection, and understanding. While modern medical research is helping us understand the physical, mental, and emotional functions of the pineal gland, spiritual adepts from the ancient mystery schools have always been aware of its benefits and wonderful etheric gifts.

The pineal gland is associated with the spiritual

nature of women and men. It is the organ of inner vision, spiritual insight, and cognition. The ancient wisdom that comes down to us — our spiritual heritage — regards this gland as the seat of cosmic thought, inspiration, imagination, and intuition. Centering in this gland allows us to experience the eternal moment. It is the opening to other dimensions, parallel realities, and infinite seas of Light and consciousness. It is the direct link to the Universal Mind and the collective consciousness. Using this gland has facilitated the work of medicine men and women, shamans, and healers, as well as practitioners of Heart & Soul Healing.

The great Taoist, Lao Tzu, wrote that the pineal is the gateway center between Heaven and Earth, and if we concentrate on this center we can realize the oneness of all things. We have also learned from other ancient masters that the spiritual function of the pineal is activated by compassion and by following the Golden Rule — do unto others as you would have them do unto you.

Love and goodness will activate, open, and stimulate pineal function. Seventy-five percent of all medical problems are stress related. I believe that a loving heart, consideration for others, and right action and living all go a long way towards stopping the physical and spiritual calcification of the pineal gland and allows an abundant flow of melatonin, which greatly reduces stress and medical problems in our lives.

Masters of the ancient mystery schools, who taught their students how to open the pineal gland, referred to it as the Inner Eye, the Eye of Wisdom, the Eye of Insight, the Eternal Eye, and the Eye That Sees All. The pineal gland is the eye of the soul; when it is open, we can see the life of the etheric plains, thought forms, and auras, all of which ordinary sight is unable to register.

In 1993, the modern Taoist Master Mantak Chia wrote about the pineal in his book, *Awaken Healing Light of the Tao*. He points out its use for telepathic communication and states:

> When this point is opened through meditation, it opens the consciousness to truth, wisdom, benevolence, and psychic power. It also enhances latent powers of healing and the body's vibrations. This center can be used to send energies out to others, or receive them from the universe. Frequencies emanating from the Third Eye can be used to explore unknown realms for higher sources of energy.

The pineal is the point of contact through which higher energy systems surrounding our body connect. Our pineal is our connection with "All That Is," and unifies our body, mind, and soul. It is the energy center for the utilization of the Divine Light or Clear Light. When observed clairvoyantly by those with etheric sight, the energy of the pineal gland is seen as a brilliant, iridescent light. The halo seen in the paintings of saints is caused by the energetic outflow from the pineal gland when the inner eye is opened and sees the Divine Light.

The halo seen in the paintings of saints is caused by the energetic outflow from the pineal gland when the inner eye is opened and sees the Divine Light.

Taoist Master Lio Jan said, "Essential nature is spiritual vitality in the heart that manifests in the center of the brain. So when seeing is concentrated on the spot between the eyes, the light of essential nature manifests and will ... unite with eternal life to become one whole .... He further suggests that we should turn inward to the pineal, "... in order to hold onto the One ... where essential nature is cultivated, and the root from which eternal life emerges." (Lu K'uan, *Taoist Yoga*)

Modern spiritual teachers and researchers have also noted interesting qualities of the pineal gland. According to Dr. David Tansley, a radionics specialist, the pineal gland encompasses 972 small vortices. In his book, *Radionics and the Subtle Bodies of Man*, Tansley states that the pineal gland is connected to our crown chakra and is formed at the point where standing lines of light cross each other twenty-one times.

Dr. Richard Gerber, another investigator of the pineal and the author of *Vibrational Medicine*, shares the following information about the pineal:

> The pineal gland is the crystalline structure that receives information from the soul and the subtle bodies, particularly the astral body. The subtle bodies often act as filters for teaching from the soul and the Higher Self. From the pineal gland, information travels to the right portion of the brain. If there is need to alert the conscious mind to this higher information, it passes through the right brain in the form of dreams. Then the left brain analyzes it to see if the information can be grasped. This often occurs

with clear dreams that offer messages. From the left brain, information travels through the neurological system, specifically passing through two critical reflex points — the medulla oblongata [in the brain] and the coccyx [at the bottom of the spine]. There is a constant state of resonance along the spinal column between the medulla oblongata and the coccyx. Properties of the pineal gland resonate between these two points.

Dr. Gerber further states:

> The crown chakra is also closely linked with the pineal gland .... For the crown chakra to be fully awakened, there must first occur a balancing of body, mind and spirit. In the individual who has an opened crown chakra, the [chakra] is represented by an energy polarity between the pineal gland and the right and left cerebral hemispheres.

By being in your pineal and practicing the Living Light Breath, you will find you no longer energetically loop with others or run energy the way you have in the past; every experience will be full-bodied.

You will develop your senses to understand and feel in a different way. Centering in the pineal does not mean you will be "in your head." Truly being in the pineal

---

By being in your pineal and practicing the Living Light Breath™ ... every experience will be full-bodied.

allows full-bodied, simultaneous alignment with all your chakras, as well as every one of the 100 trillion cells within your body.

From the pineal there are some 366 senses you will be able to develop and explore. You will be able to choose what to energetically experience in your life.

Chapter 23

The Hara Point

The Hara point is an important energy center in the body. In Chinese medicine this area is called the "Medicine Field" because of the curative power of the energies gathered there. The body uses this energy to function normally. When doing the Living Light Breath (Chapter 24), we activate and strengthen the energy in the Hara by drawing energy from Source to this center. It is a place in the body where you can unify the physical, mental, emotional, and spiritual bodies.

The Hara is located about one and a half inches behind the navel and is the exact point of balance in the body. If you were suspended from this point by a wire, your body would be perfectly balanced horizontally.

The modern Taoist Master Mantak Chia writes in his book, *Awaken the Healing Light of the Tao*, about the importance of the Hara point or what he calls the navel center:

> The navel area was our first connection with the outside world. All oxygen, blood, and nutrients flowed into our fetal forms through this abdominal doorway. As a result, the navel center has a special sensitivity that continues far beyond the cutting of the umbilical cord at birth; it stays with us throughout our entire lives. The navel is the physical center of the body, halfway between the upper and lower body. In mar-

tial arts, calligraphy, and other related disciplines, one often hears of the importance of centering. The center of the body, our center of gravity, is the most effective place from which to coordinate one's movements, and in these arts one learns to move from one's center, which is called the Lower Tan Tien in Chinese, or Hara in Japanese.

When practicing the Living Light Breath, you bring energy to the Hara and can begin to use that center for spiritual transformation. Building a strong spiritual foundation by consciously fortifying and activating the light in the Hara was a basic exercise of the ancient mystery schools. Chia calls this area the "storage battery," because it collects, transforms, and balances energies taken in from other sources.

Noted healer, Barbara Brennan, also writes about the qualities and importance of the Hara point:

> The Hara exists on a dimension deeper than the auric field. It exists on the level of intentionality. It is an area of power within the physical body that contains the tan tien (the gate of life). It is the one note with which you draw up your physical body from your mother, the earth. It is this one note that holds your body in physical manifestation. Without the one note, you would not have a body. When you change this one note, your entire body will change. Your body is a gelatinous form held together by this one note. This note is the sound the center of the earth makes.

The Hara is the second mind or brain in the body, sometimes called "the abdominal brain." In Chinese medicine this area is also called "The Mind Palace" (Shen Ch'ue). Western medical researchers have recently confirmed what the ancient ones have known for a long-time; Neurogastroenterology is now a field of study.

On January 23, 1996, the New York Times alerted its readers about the Enteric Nervous System or abdominal brain. Eric Yudelove, author of *The Tao and the Tree of Life*, recently summarized this article. In writing about the "gut brain" and the findings of the medical researchers, he says:

> The Enteric Nervous System is a second nervous system within our body, separate and apart from the Central Nervous System. According to the New York Times article, both nervous systems have a common source in the embryo. A clump of tissue called the Neural Crest forms early in the development of the embryo. One section of the Neural Crest develops into the Central Nervous System. A second portion splits away and migrates to form the Enteric Nervous System. For a time in the embryo's development, the two systems exist independent of each other. Later they are joined together by the Vagus Nerve. Until recently it was thought that the brain in our heads controlled the abdominal muscles and sensory nerves. This now turns out not to be true; this area is controlled by the Enteric Nervous System or Abdominal Brain.
>
> The Enteric Nervous system is located within the sheets of tissue lining the esopha-

gus, stomach, small and large intestines. There is an interaction between the two brains, when one get upset the other one does too. For example when you are worried, you are prone to getting an upset stomach. The Abdominal Brain can effect the Central Nervous System as well. Usually this takes the form of negative messages of pain and discomfort accompanied by a lot of chatter in the head whose source you never seem to be able to locate. Let me quote the article, 'The brain in the gut plays a major role in human happiness and misery. But few people know it exists.'

Yudelove goes on to explain that the Vagus Nerve is also connected to the main organs in the body. When we draw light to the Hara point, or Abdominal Mind, we are also helping ourselves to energize the entire body. The first seven breaths of the Living Light Breath are drawn into the Hara. In the eight breath we center in the pineal gland and connect the physical, mental, emotional, and spiritual bodies with the Universal Mind and the collective consciousness.

Chapter 24

The Living Light Breath™

I made an important discovery several years ago when I was in Florida teaching a workshop. During the class, I did a Heart & Soul Healing session with a volunteer. In her session, she went to a past life when she was watching Christ being crucified on the cross. She talked about witnessing Christ's death. Being an empath, I asked the class if they would like to experience what it felt like for Christ to leave his body. The class and the volunteer agreed and I moved into that place.

Two thousand years ago a gate was created by the Christ being, Jesus of Nazareth. This gate connects the body and the spirit, the realms above and the realms below, and the inner worlds with the outer worlds. It was created and opened to all human consciousness at the time of his death. The gate was specifically activated as Christ took his last physical breath and moved into the Living Light Breath and Unity Consciousness.

I was able to feel this last physical breath. As Christ died, his head dropped down towards his chest. There was a moment of silence, and then it felt as though something was pulling him straight out of his body. As I continued to follow Christ energetically, I realized his vibration had created a gate or portal to access Source. I became aware that all we had to do was love ourselves as much as this master loved himself, and through that vibration we could access this gate. This is the same vibration that Buddha and many other ascended masters utilized. This vibrational state is not about religion; it is about self-love and the oneness of Source.

The gate is activated every time an ascended master takes his last breath and moves into the unity consciousness grid. The Living Light Breath is a way to move into this grid and connect with all living consciousness everywhere. It brings this connection into our physical awareness through the pineal gland.

THE LIVING LIGHT BREATH: BASIC BREATHING LOGISTICS

The complete breath consists of three natural, specific states of focus: inhalation, retention (a holding or pause state), and exhalation. The logistics of the Living Light Breath are as follows:

- Sit erect with your spine comfortably straight.
- Place your hands in your lap in a mudra position. I suggest you touch the tips of each index finger to your thumbs. Use any mudra, however, that feels natural to you. The purpose of this is to keep energy from blowing out your hands.
- During the entire breath sequence, keep your tongue flat, touching the roof of your mouth above your teeth. Keeping your tongue on the roof of your mouth connects the two major meridians in your body and prevents any energy from blowing out your crown chakra or between your legs. When you are not speaking, it is a good energy practice to always keep your tongue on the roof of your mouth. By doing so, a person can gain as much as twenty to thirty percent more energy, which previously was lost.
- Double lock your anus. This is accomplished by first locking the opening to your anus by squeezing the muscles of your buttocks together. This is the first lock.

92

- The second lock is accomplished by pretending there is a string coming out of your belly button. At the same time you are locking the opening to the anus, pull that string. As you pull it, your belly will be pulled inward. This double lock prevents any energy from being lost from the Hara point.
- Close your eyes, breathe through your nose, and relax.
- Begin the Living Light Breath by consciously drawing in a deep cleansing breath through your mouth. Now completely release this breath, fully relaxing your body and letting go of everything. Wait. Some people may feel a mild tugging sensation like you are being pulled out of your body through a tube. If you notice this sensation, stay physically in your body.
- Breathe through your nose and up through this tube. Then bring the breath back down, centering it in your Hara point (without exhaling). Remember the Hara point is an inch and a half behind the belly button.
- Now double lock your anus, holding your breath as long as is comfortable.
- Exhale through your nose, releasing the lock.
- On the next breath once again imagine you are breathing up the tube.
- Again bring the breath down to the Hara point. Double lock. Each time you exhale release the lock.
- Continue to breathe in this manner seven times, extending the breath further upward on each breath until it reaches the sun. Imagine your breath traveling up the tube on your in-breath, bringing in the light of Source. Continue bringing your breath down into your Hara point and hold it for as long as it is comfortable, without straining. Release the lock each time.
- On the eighth breath, as you exhale, release the double

lock and keep these locks relaxed thereafter. As you breathe up the tube, bring your center to your pineal gland in the center of your head.

- Hold your breath as long as comfortable. Continue to breathe up the tube, centering in your pineal, for about five minutes. From your pineal gland, you now will be able to connect to all your chakras in a new way.

Consider making this way of breathing a part of your daily life. Let it become a part of who you are. Do this breath each morning so you can have the benefit of this energy and clarity throughout the day. The ideal state would be to stay centered in your pineal, breathing from that place all the time. In addition, breathing from the pineal allows you to consciously become a part of unity consciousness. Breathing this breath enables you to move into the timeless space of the moment and stay present and aware while connected consciously to the Creator. Breathing the Living Light Breath is the quickest, easiest, and most harmonious way to bring the aspect of INscension into your body and integrate it into your way of being.

For those of you who would like further information, I have a video, *Living Light Breath — Gateway to Unity Consciousness*. Please refer to the back of this book for ordering information.

Breathing the Living Light Breath™
is the quickest, easiest, and most
harmonious way to bring the aspect of
INscension™ into your body and
integrate it into your way of being.

Chapter 25

The Way It Works

For thousands of years there has been an elite group who controlled certain information about religious mysteries and God. This group was made up of those in power: shamans, priests, religious leaders, the intellectual elite, ruling class, and government. Their knowledge was kept secret, given out very slowly, or modified as a way of keeping the common man from knowing the complete truth.

In the past, because of a lack of education, a focus on survival, and a tendency to give our power away to those who say they have the answers, we have been quick to believe our leaders. This led to wars, prejudice, and hatred between people, races, and countries. We came to rely on certain people or groups to have the answers for us — usually religions or governments. These leaders were the appointed prophets of our time.

There are many groups of people today, including governments, who believe that if we knew the truth about technology, extra terrestrial beings, mind control, our true origins, or hundreds of other topics our society, culture, and government would break down. This lack of knowledge creates confusion about our true nature — who we are and why we are here — and our concept of Source.

We are overloaded with information today, challenging the core of who and what we are. The Internet and twenty-four hour news programs instantly connect us to the whole world, and we are saturated with information and looking for answers to what it all means.

I recently received a letter from a well-known spiritual teacher. This letter went out to many different countries and contained bits and pieces of information detailing the end of the world. I began to receive calls from people who were alarmed and wondering what they should do. Most of them were afraid to do anything at all. They wanted to be saved.

Fear can never create beneficial change. Many people dwell on fearful ideas, and it pulls them out of the moment, keeping them in the past or projecting them into a scary future. I am concerned that if enough people give their fears so much energy, their ideas could become a physical manifestation.

At times like this, gurus or prophets step in. Historically, when these types of scenarios were prophesied but did not occur, one of these prophets commonly came forth to tell us they had enlisted the help of their guides, angels, or supernatural powers to step in and save us. As a result, many of us have pledged our undying love and support to these "saviors."

It is important to know these changes are really nothing new. I have followed this same information closely for a number of years. During the last six months of 1998, the Art Bell radio show (www.artbell.com) focused on this type of material. New speakers came on nightly, adding their ideas and opinions about what was to come. They had projections about everything from the Y2K situation

---

We are overloaded with information today, challenging the core of who and what we are.

---

to new renditions of Nostradamus' prophecies. Gordon Michael Scallion, Ed Dames, Stan Deyo, Sean David Morton, Richard Hogland, Gregg Braden, Whitley Streiber, Robert Ghost Wolf, and for the first time in history, the Hopi Elders, as well as many others, offered their views on upcoming events. They all had the same message: Change is upon us.

Many of us forget the importance of discernment. There can be three of us with different ideas and each will create a unique scenario. What we believe and focus on will become our reality. These cycles of change, which seem so new and frightening, have always been occurring. This is the first time, however, that we have been exposed to so much information about these changes all at once. On any given day, for example, approximately twenty to thirty earthquakes occur around the world, but until the arrival of instant communication most of us were unaware of them.

Millions of people throughout history have died because of man made and natural causes, including disease, war, and earth changes. We heard about most of these catastrophic disasters after the fact, safe with knowing it did not happen to us. In late summer of 1998, floods affected over 250 million people in China. These people lost their homes, their incomes, and everything they owned. Yet, in the United States, we heard very little about this disaster. If this had happened in the United States, it would have impacted almost everyone. Our world would certainly have changed. Would we

---

Many of us forget the importance of discernment.

have taken it as a sign the world was coming to an end?

I do not believe the Earth will be destroyed. I do not believe there will be mass death and destruction. My knowing says these times can be a gentle transition — a time of grace and ease in the midst of change.

So what can you do during this time to create choices and ease the transition? I choose to stay physically active. I play, relax, eat properly, and drink lots of water. I spend time with people I care about, the land, and animals. I swim, enjoy the water, and, most importantly, explore my passions.

Passion is a key word. What excites you? What brings the spark of life into your being? Once you find what this is, enjoy it as often as you can.

I feel my personal energetics, and the energetics around me, are changing. As the electromagnetic fields change, our emotional, spiritual, and mental bodies are moving closer and closer to our physical body. Anything we are holding on to or have not resolved from our past is causing our physical reality to become energetically distorted. I believe these times are focusing on the collapse of time and our old emotional beliefs. I hope the information in this book has helped you enjoy that journey.

"Letting go" is extremely important. Let go of what no longer serves you, such as past emotions, old relationships, and the way you have been in the past. Let go of worrying about the way you look. Let go of how you think other people should be and judgments you have about yourself and others. Anything you are holding onto in these times of change will intensify your physical reality.

We are creating differently now than in the past and this is confusing. Working harder, sacrificing, and doing things as before no longer brings results. I believe the reason for this is we are all moving into instantaneous creation. We are experiencing the collapse of everything around us that is not true to and supportive of our heart and spirit. This is what will happen when we become "conscious," which brings with it a sense of knowing and security. The closer we move into instantaneous creation, the clearer we need to be about what we are choosing to create in our lives.

Loving, exploring what love means for us, and opening up more than we ever have before is where we are moving now. It is necessary to move through the veil of illusion and fear and be totally exposed — to love yourself so much that you have pure love and compassion for yourself and all those around you. We are now coming together as family, as the soul of oneness, with no separation.

The closer we move into instantaneous creation, the clearer we need to be about what we are choosing to create in our lives.

Ken Page

Heart & Soul Healing™
Institute of Multidimensional Cellular Healing™

The Third Eye of Horus Mystery School™

1158 Highway 105,
Boone, North Carolina 28607

Toll free in U.S.: (800) 809-1290
Tel: (828) 263-0330, Fax: (828) 264-4757

e-mail: ken@kenpage.com

www.kenpage.com

Ask for Ken's free monthly e-mail newsletter.

Please check Ken's web site or contact the Institute for information on upcoming events, Heart & Soul Healing sessions, weekend workshops, and Practitioner training classes.

Information about Your Heart & Soul Healing Session

Combining Physical, Emotional, Mental, and Spiritual Realities

Heart & Soul Healing™ (HSH™) is a powerful way to discover your truth. Its purpose is to assist you by integrating your whole being with your Higher Self.

In your session, Ken looks for patterns your conscious mind is not aware of, but that your subconscious mind is giving energy. Your subconscious mind knows everything that has ever happened to you, all your realities and experiences since the time you came from the Creator. If there is a current inner conflict, it can be found, understood, and released. Protection from outer influences and energies comes with greater awareness and understanding, as well as accepting full responsibility for your intentions, emotions, desires, thoughts, and actions.

No matter how much work we may have done to understand our mental, emotional, spiritual, and physical issues, there is often a missing piece that stops our final resolution of an issue. As a result, patterns are created over and over in our lives to have yet another chance to gain the wisdom, understanding, and knowledge of our lessons. In addition, any fears or emotional residue we may be holding about a particular issue throws further confusion over the problem, making it almost impossible to see the bigger picture.

HSH addresses ways our inner mind assists us to understand self-made barriers. It is a unique resource to help us understand events and experiences beyond the physical, assisting us in our growth as we reestablish connection to our Higher Self.

Ken has performed thousands of private and remote sessions, and recognizes the power of the inner mind in overcoming and releasing spiritual, mental, emotional, and physical problems. He is committed to assisting you in the discovery of your inner truth and the reasons behind unresolved issues and reoccurring patterns in your life.

KEY POINTS OF A HEART & SOUL HEALING SESSION

When Ken begins your session, discovering the collective consciousness that you are balancing is extremely important. The primary energy that you are balancing needs to be dealt with at the beginning of your work together so that other techniques used later in the session are not distorted. Once you find the primary energy and are able to balance it, your vibration changes, and you will stop attracting that energy into your life.

At some point in your life, or in a past life, you became connected with the energy of a collective consciousness. This connection is often made because of a promise you made, such as "I am going to do something about war" or "I am going to do something about sadness." Discovering what these promises are, promises made perhaps fifteen past lives ago, will show you that you are actually a part of what you have been creating. You are not a victim of your life, but a creator and a creator on multi-levels of reality.

It is important that you understand, spiritually, mentally, emotionally, and physically, your role in balancing this collective consciousness — and there may be more than one that you are working with. It shows the unique role that you are playing in the energetics of this planet

102

and adds another dimension to why you are here on Earth at this time in history. It is important for you to know that you have been doing your soul work all along, even if you were not consciously aware of it.

If you do not understand your role on multidimensions of reality to balance various collective consciousnesses of energy, you may feel very frustrated about your life path because you have not found the vehicle of understanding that shows you that you are really who you think they are.

In your session, besides understanding the collective consciousness that you have agreed to help balance in this lifetime, you will also find pieces of you that are out of time. Ken believes that we are all one — that there are trillions of cells that represent your body and resonate with every other cell in every other person.

Here you are, living in the moment, but do your thoughts dwell on your past? We often think about the past so much that it distorts the present moment, and we are no longer fully present in our bodies now. These pieces of you out of time could be fragments from a past life that have not completely integrated with you. Ken will assist you to bring everything back into balance with who you are today. As you do this, you will heal yourself and change your vibration.

Finding pieces that are attached to you is another key part of your session. The word "attached" sounds alarming, but what if these attachments are just people, or the souls of people, that you have loved in the past. These people are energetically still looped or corded with you today, and they are using your energy even though they might not be in your life in the way they were. Remember, we use others to reflect back to us who we are, and we constantly do this when we interact. Perhaps you do not realize the amount of energy you use to engage with and connect with these energetic attachments.

The fourth area you will look at in your session is past lives or past times where key programs were set. If you have a subconscious program that you are giving energy to that says it is not safe to love, or take your power or be who you are, then that program limits your world.

Ken always asks his clients how much energy they are using to keep themselves from being happy and most people tell him they are using 50–75% of their energy. They have a program that says: If I am happy and have everything I want — everything that I could ever imagine or desire — someone will take it away from me. The other program that seems to go with it is: I will hurt myself so that nobody else will hurt me.

You cannot get to these past-life programs unless you have cleared the primary energy, brought the pieces of you that are out of time back into alignment, and disconnected the way you have looped with others energetically in the past. You also must clear the patterns and energy you are holding in your nervous system and the fluid in your spine and brain. If these areas are not cleared beforehand, the past-life programs you have will be distorted by these other energies, and it will take many, many sessions before you get to the heart of the problem.

At the end of your session with Ken, he will bring back and integrate the part of you that left around the age of three years old when you said, "I do not want to be here." Ken believes this child part of your spirit or soul separated from your body and has been witnessing or observing you from outside of yourself all these years. Integrating this child vibration and bringing back into alignment all the different pieces of you that have been out of time and caught up in distortions, is called INscension. Being all one allows you to experience the moment in a whole different way and changes your reality and your vibration as you continue, empowered, on your soul path.

——— PRIVATE AND REMOTE TELEPHONE ——— SESSIONS WITH KEN PAGE

- How many times have you suffered for speaking your truth?
- How many times have you been hurt for helping others?
- What decisions have you made based on these past experiences, and are they still affecting you today?

Some of the experiences you may have during your session with Ken:

- Discover the collective consciousness that you are balancing
- Discover your mission and purpose for being here now
- Discover and integrate pieces of you that are out of time or held in past emotions
- Release karmic attachments you still have to parents, lovers, or others
- Release conflicting programs in your subconscious: It is not safe to love. It is not safe to be in my power. It is not safe to be who I am.
- Experience INscension and bring that feeling into all of your body now
- Energetically clear your chakras and meridian points

- Identify symbols to unlock information from your past
- Release energetic patterns you are carrying from past traumas
- Learn what energies or patterns you picked up from your parents
- Connect with Source in a way you can repeat after your session
- Release psychic weight you are holding due to your subconscious thoughts
- Bring in the parts of you which have not felt safe to be here until now
- Balance and release all thoughts out of balance with your nervous system and internal organs
- Discover how to be present and exceed your potential
- Learn how to connect to your Higher Self
- Uncover what has been interfering with your prosperity and creativity
- Clarify the reason for your reoccurring patterns
- Reintegrate any soul fragments and separated parts of your personality
- Gain freedom from destructive emotions and programming
- Understand lessons from past lifetimes

Common issues addressed in a session are:

Low energy, fears without cause, relationship and health issues, unbreakable habits, low self-esteem, chronic pain, connections with ETs and multidimensional aspects, sexual abuse, and karmic and traumatic links to the past.

Call the Institute or check our web site for workshop details and a schedule of events. If you have a group and would be interested in sponsoring a workshop in your area, please contact the Institute for a sponsor packet.

The Art of Heaven on Earth Workshops
Third Eye of Horus Mystery School Teachings

In January 1997, the Third Eye of Horus Mystery School was reactivated in the King's Chamber of the Great Pyramid on the Giza Plateau in Egypt. The Third Eye of Horus Mystery School teachings unify the right and left eye mystery wisdom. The left eye of Horus teachings develop mental acuity and clarity. The right eye of Horus teachings clear emotional distortion so that you can fully utilize your passionate, emotional, and creative powers.

These blended teachings allow you to open all of your hidden senses and to bring these sensory abilities to conscious awareness, along with information from Source, resulting in the achievement of Unity Consciousness and living a life of balance, clarity, joy, love, and compassion.

At this time on Earth, all information is collapsing onto this very moment. There are no longer any secrets. Ken will guide and support you in understanding this knowledge and give you simple techniques that you can use after the workshop to help you continue your empowerment, understanding, and clear access to your Higher Self.

Do you know how energy works in your life and in your relationships? Are you the master of what you create? Ken will share secrets of ancient mystery schools that he has written about in his latest book, *The Heart of Soul Healing*. He will give you spiritual techniques — never shown before — to assist you in achieving the highest and purest vibration available within yourself. This experience will support you in attracting and creating a more positive, healthy, and abundant life.

Through stories and demonstrations, Ken will help you find your own self-empowerment and oneness with your Higher Self. You will also receive, The Way It Works, Ken's popular technique handbook.

If you are looking for a positive life, better relationships, abundance, and a healthy way of being in your body and soul, do not miss this exciting workshop. A time for personal, in-depth exploration.

Heart & Soul Healing Practitioner Training

The five-day HSH Practitioner Training is an experiential workshop designed to prepare you to clear and balance yourself, as well as learn, understand, and practice the techniques of HSH.

This course is offered several times a year in the United States and abroad. Ken will personally instruct students in his healing technique, as well as share his latest ideas and theories.

Students will observe complete client sessions, highlighting the latest techniques. You will also have the opportunity to practice sessions of your own in class.

At course completion, you will be certified as a HSH Practitioner and will be listed on Ken's web site, if you wish.

Please see Ken's web site or call the Institute for details and locations.

www.kenpage.com

Prerequisites for the course:

- Private or Remote Heart & Soul Healing session with Ken Page
- One-day workshop with Ken or viewing of the workshop video series (contact the Institute for information)

Thorough knowledge of the following books:
- *The Heart of Soul Healing*
- *The Way It Works*
- *HSH Philosophy and Application Manual*
- *The End of Time*

- Viewing of the Animal Healing video
- Holographic Healing Tones and Sacred Sounds or Sacred Tones & Earth Music with Dolphins and Whales audio
- Written completion of the review questions in HSH Philosophies & Applications Manual
- Practice of the Clearing Techniques
- Practice of the Living Light Breath

The Heart of Soul Healing
The Traveler Series
by Ken Page

When Spirit called Ken to lead a conscious life, he journeyed into unknown territories. Comfortable in the corporate world as an entrepreneur and business-man, he entered a multidimensional world of wonder, delight, magic, miracles, transformation, and healing.

As a spiritual healer, Ken became the full-time confidante of people's private thoughts, hidden secrets, and spiritual yearnings. He discovered hidden wisdom in the stories of his clients. They showed Ken why we are here and why our lives unfold in so many different ways.

The *Heart of Soul Healing* has been Ken's focus and passion for the last fifteen years. He shares everything that he has learned on his healing journey to date. The philosophy, development, and practice of Heart & Soul Healing, the transformational process Ken developed working with his clients' inner spiritual and energetic worlds, is the main focus, but also important is the story of Ken's search for the soul — why Ken needed to search, where this led him, and his surprising discovery.

The process of Heart & Soul Healing (formerly called Multidimensional Cellular Healing™) is a unique way of tapping into the subconscious truth inside each of us. Included in this book are case studies that portray the healing transformation that we can all experience. In these stories, the strength and courage of each human spirit shines through in spite of sometimes sad and horrific experiences. These people revealed their divine natures as they persevered until they understood themselves and their creations. It is Ken's hope that the courage, desire, and drive portrayed in these stories will inspire you as they have him.

The *Heart of Soul Healing* is a text book for practitioners of the healing arts. Alternative healers, psychologists, doctors, ministers, counselors, parents, and all those in search of God and Spirit will find this book invaluable, because its healing wisdom is universal.

Over 400 pages including in depth case studies and step by step instructions. Illustrated.

ISBN 0-9649703-2-5 $39.95

Heart & Soul Healing™ Philosophy and Applications Manual

A working manual detailing some of the basic principles behind *Heart & Soul Healing*. Includes detailed information about energetics, creatorship, accessing the holographic whole brain, and moving beyond the senses and out of dualities. This manual also includes exploration of the major modalities of learning, understanding relationships, altered states, symbols, and working with the animal kingdom. A prerequisite to HSH Practitioner Training classes.

ISBN 0-9649703-3-3 $19.95

The Traveler and The End of Time
The Secret Life of Ken Page

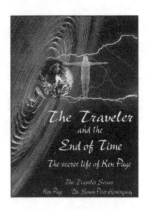

Contains dozens of fascinating and inspiring true stories from the life of Ken Page. Starting with his humble beginnings as a seven-year-old entrepreneur and continuing through his years as a millionaire businessman, Ken's story culminates in a dramatic series of miracles, tragedies, and triumphs all leading to his successful healing practice today.

ISBN 0-9649703-1-7 $11.95

The Traveler Ken Page and The Fallen Angel

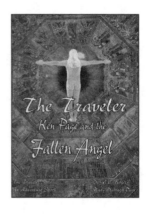

The touching and riveting story of Ken Page, his wife Mary, and her former husband Daniel, who came to live with them. Join Ken and Daniel as they search for a meaning to life that speaks to your heart, and most importantly, to your soul. This 90s version of the "Search for the Holy Grail" will hold your imagination from beginning to end.

ISBN 0-9649703-0-9 $11.95

Six Video Set: The Heart of Soul Healing
Two-day Workshop with Ken Page

For over twelve years, Ken Page has worked on his new book, *The Heart of Soul Healing*, which is now complete. This is the first time Ken has shared all of his techniques, gathered from working with thousands of people.

In his workshop, Ken will share this special healing process, which allows you to access your physical, mental, emotional and spiritual bodies and create the life you choose for yourself!

$200.00 US

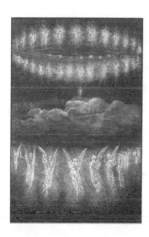

Living Light Breath™
Gateway to Unity
Consciousness

Two thousand years ago a gate was created by the Christ being, Jesus of Nazareth. This gate connects the body and the spirit, the realms above and the realms below, and the inner worlds with the outer worlds. It was created and opened to all human consciousness at the time of his death. The gate was activated as Christ took his last physical breath and moved into the Living Light Breath and Unity Consciousness. $19.95

Animal Healing and Clearing

Ken demonstrates his healing work with animals by showing you how to clear and balance a cat, dog, and horse. He also discusses techniques for fully experiencing nature, both energetically and spiritually. $19.95

An Introduction to the Work of Ken Page

A thirty-minute television interview of Ken discussing Multidimensional Cellular Healing (now called Heart & Soul Healing.) $14.95

An Introduction to Ken Page and Heart & Soul Healing (formerly called Multidimensional Cellular Healing™)

A sixty-minute audiotape of Ken discussing his work and philosophy.

$5.00

Sacred Tones and Earth Music with Dolphins and Whales

A sixty-minute audiotape of Ken Page using tones with the dolphins and whales. Original music by Barry Oser incorporates Ken's energy balancing tones.

$9.95

Holographic Healing Tones and Sacred Sounds

A sixty-minute audiotape of Ken Page using sound to shift and clear cellular imprints. Tones change energy patterns, releasing old imprints.

$9.95

Shipping and handling charges in the United States:

Under $10 = $3.00, $10.01 – $20 = $4.00, $20.01 – $50 = $5.00, $50.01 – $149 = $6.00, over $150 = $8.00

Call for foreign shipping charges.

We have one hundred trillion cells. Each cell represents another consciousness; we are all reflected inside of each other. If you want to help another person, go inside yourself and love that person as he or she exists inside of you. We are able to do this more effectively when we become love — when we unconditionally love all one hundred trillion parts of ourselves. If you want to pray to the Creator, be love, go inside, and address your prayers to your internal divine presence.

I have dedicated my life to my truth, compassion, and unconditional love.

If you have enjoyed this information please tell your friends and send them a book.

Ken Page

Love what you don't like. (Your belly)
for 30 seconds at a time -
2 min. a day.

We choose people
who reflect our issues.
Do you 'need' your
past to define you?

We are on the
leading edge } "becoming
conscious!"

USA - 4% } pop of world
.0001 } are interested

are you a creator or victim?
are we 'one' or 'separate'?

But - - - -

"Energetic Clearing" Technique
choice of what you feel or
don't feel.